CHARLESTON SAVED
1979–1989

CHARLESTON SAVED
1979–1989

'One of the most difficult and
imaginative feats of restoration …'

Anthea Arnold

Robert Hale • London

© Anthea Arnold 2010
First published in Great Britain 2010

ISBN 978-0-7090-9018-2

Robert Hale Limited
Clerkenwell House
Clerkenwell Green
London EC1R 0HT

www.halebooks.com

A catalogue record for this book is available from the British Library

2 4 6 8 10 9 7 5 3 1

Typeset by Dave Jones
Printed in Great Britain by the MPG Books Group, Bodmin and King's Lynn

Preface

The many hundreds of visitors who come to look at the house and garden today should be reminded that, had it not been for Debo Gage and the serendipity of her coming back to this country and looking for a cottage in the area, all this might not exist at all and would certainly not be as it is now. She was a young businesswoman in the art world, and she used all her skills and all her energy, without stint, and without financial reward, to bring this about. She once wrote, 'When I do something I put my heart into it 100%' – I hope this book bears witness to that.

I hope also that it will give recognition to the many others who gave so much to Charleston, especially those who did the work on the house and wrote about it in 1987. The book was never published but the Foreword by Simon Watney and Epilogue by Angelica Garnett are reprinted here and the words written by the others have been used throughout.

A.A.

Contents

The Ethos of Charleston

Charleston farmhouse could so easily have vanished into obscurity. We embarked upon our campaign to the daunting backdrop of a recession and an 'anti-Blooms-bury' backlash. As Charleston became one of the first 'modern' houses to be saved in England, we experienced great cynicism. However, in a small way we threw a pebble into the pond, whose ripples have since spread, resulting in the National Trust taking on Erno Goldfinger's house, 2 Willow Road, John Lennon's home in Liver-pool, and others such as William Morris's Red House.

The saving of Charleston and its first restoration between 1979 and 1989 will resonate today and tomorrow. It was an extraordinary achievement, carried out by individuals who devoted their hearts and unstinting time to the task. It was this conviction and passion that saved Charleston. The work of many of them is chron-icled in the pages of this book. There were, of course, dozens of others involved who sadly cannot all be thanked individually. Looking back, it is amazing how many people came forward and in countless ways galvanized our mission to raise money. All these events needed notices, which were usually designed by Angelica Garnett. A mailing list required collating and envelopes needed stuffing. These jobs were repeatedly undertaken by a team of boundlessly enthusiastic volunteers. During the early 'finding our way days' Charleston was very much run off the top of a kitchen table – or a succession of kitchen tables.

The case for saving Charleston farmhouse was summed up by Quentin Bell in the autumn of 1979, when I first met him and suggested that the house and its contents should be saved. I asked him to write a piece for our press release; in just a few para-graphs he captured its essence. From my perspective, a very intriguing aspect of this project was the fact that were we to have restored an eighteenth-century property, it would have involved a degree of educated guesswork. However, the integrity of Charleston is that it was a complete 'time capsule' from the Bronco toilet paper to the Bakelite electrical fittings. Importantly, we drew upon the experience of living family members, to ensure accuracy in capturing an immensely personal lifestyle and its *raison d'être* as an artists' home.

My own barometer was largely derived from the family, Quentin and Olivier Bell and Angelica Garnett, who were truly generous with their time and insight. End-lessly we discussed and explored every possible aspect of Charleston, since we were concerned with a fragile and tangible spirit. Often, I realized that I was treading a very delicate tightrope of feelings and questioned whether it was right to ask Quentin, Olivier, Angelica and their families to consider making the personal and financial sacrifices they have over the years. This was never far from my mind. I recall one Open Day at Charleston following the first phase of the reopening of the house after restoration. I was standing at the back of the marquee listening to the speeches when suddenly I felt a big hug. I turned around to discover that it was Angelica. Taken by surprise, I thought it was an embrace of farewell. 'Oh, are you leaving?' I said. 'No' she replied, 'I simply wanted to thank you.' Relief flooded over me. It is my hope and desire that succeeding generations will always be a part of this unique place.

Bringing together all the pieces encompassed by a project of this nature over a decade, I found myself talking to a great number of people, either from a practical standpoint or simply to put forward our case for recognition and funding. In the process of convincing myself, so that I could convey to others the validity of our cause, I found myself enormously struck by a speech given by Colin Thompson, the Director of the National Galleries of Scotland, in the early 1980s, on the subject of the conservation of our cultural heritage. His subject, 'Preservation vs change – are they compatible?' struck a profound chord in me. There is no point in saving a place if it is to be changed in the process, for example by becoming a shrine. Here lies the challenge.

The essence of Charleston has always been about the tempering of new ideas. In this respect, I feel immensely proud that thanks to the heights the Charleston Festival, organized by Diana Reich, has now attained, Charleston continues to be a touchstone for current thought, literature and artistic ideas, and thus its inimitable tradition persists.

I also applaud the leadership that followed my work, and has accomplished the most difficult task of all: providing for Charleston's financial underpinning and future stability. Raising money for bricks and mortar is easier than for endowment and maintenance. There will always be a need for fundraising, simply to cope with rising costs and inflation before one even takes the other objectives of the Charleston Trust into account. Likewise, the conservation of Charleston is a continuing process, and a second restoration programme was put into effect, led by Alastair Upton and its curator, Wendy Hitchmough, to safeguard the collection for the future and make the house more accessible. This project started in March 2003, almost twenty years after the first restoration, and was supported by the Heritage Lottery Fund.

On this theme, I do have a message. It is my belief that the ultimate 'litmus test' of the integrity of our achievement, and how the future will come to judge it, is the way in which the house is shown and accessed, and the number of visitors who visit it at any one time. A large enough endowment is the key, thereby mitigating the reliance on income from entry fees. The soul of Charleston is its atmosphere, its quirky, fragile ambience. This unique experience is only possible if each visitor's encounter is intimate. If it is, our *real* challenge will have been accomplished.

Charleston is and always has been about experimentation.

Deborah Gage
London, July 2009

Foreword

Already in the last few years of Duncan Grant's life, Charleston seemed to be quietly folding in upon itself. No longer able to manage the stairs up to his own bedroom, he took to sleeping in Vanessa Bell's room, next to his studio, with its French windows opening onto the garden, which she had tended with so much love. In the years after Duncan's death I only visited Charleston two or three times. The leaves of the huge magnolia grandiflora still scratched the windows of Clive Bell's bedroom, and the sounds of farmyard animals and distant hammering drifted indoors. But, for the first time since Duncan and Vanessa had taken up residence in 1916, there was no creative work going on. These were uniquely depressing visits.

Walking back up the lane to Charleston in 1986 to attend a meeting of the Trust – my first – I realized how much I dreaded going back. I dreaded the musty air of the mausoleum of cultism and cultural taxidermy. At the same time I realized how much I had missed Duncan's Charleston through the intervening years and how I had protected myself against my feelings by cutting loose and simply staying away. I was astonished. Charleston was filled with life – to my great surprise and relief. This I could never have imagined. There were changes, of course, but the house had recovered its essential integrity. So much work had been done, so much skill and care lavished on its every last surface and detail. It was as if the mere presence of laughter and music and talking had unleashed a genie within the very fabric of the building; as if, basking in this new recognition of the beauty of its decorations, Charleston had restored itself, its stuffs and painted walls and furniture resaturated not just with the warmth of their original colours, but with an intelligence of their original purpose and the pleasure of their making.

Now Charleston is open to everyone, and I think its extraordinary success as a place to visit lies exactly in this new sense of mission – to inspire a lively and enlarging awareness of the possible, in both aesthetic and social terms. It is not a museum but a manifesto, embodying an approach to decorative art which is still as challenging to the 'ghastly good taste' of today as it was to the fussily timid sensibilities of the Edwardian era. Charleston is something of a rough diamond. It does not represent the polished and the finished. Its great sophistication, its wit, and its essentially unprecious elegance stand for the life and values of the extraordinary people who lived and worked there. It is that special combination of living and working which sets it apart. How easily and efficiently it gives the lie to a fashionable and silly myth in which Vanessa Bell and her household are lifted out from the unacceptable complexities of their actual working lives and social relations and elevated to the misty, imaginary stage of 'genius'.

Charleston embodies the plain common sense which lies behind Virginia Woolf's barbed comment that writing is not 'spun in thin-air by incorporeal creatures'. In this respect it is quite the reverse of the traditional British stately home, which offers its collection of pictures, furniture and fine porcelain far removed from their various sites of production and all sanctioned in the mystical names of 'Family', 'Property' and 'Nation'. Charleston is an artist's house, a house in which artists worked in a steady, ordered regime. The active feeling of *intrusion* which some visitors have described is a measure of the sense of that regime as it somehow concretely survives. This impression of intensely purposive privacy, of lives lived 'under the rose', is the essence of the place. The integrity of it thus lies against the grain, as it were, of most conservation projects. For it cannot easily be appropriated to the notion of supposedly unified national heritage. After all, it was always to some extent a place of internal exile, from the very motives which obliged Vanessa Bell to seek a home in the country in the first place. Certainly it sits very uneasily indeed against the cosy pieties of hearth and home which are celebrated in so many other county houses – the same 'Victorian values' which outraged Bloomsbury into existence in the first place and which are regrettably once more so high on the agenda of our national culture.

> One feather, and the house, sinking, falling, would have turned and pitched downwards to the depths of darkness. In the ruined room, picnickers would have lit their kettles; lovers sought shelter there, lying on the bare boards; and the shepherd stored his dinner on the bricks, and the tramp slept with his coat round him to ward off the cold. Then the roof would have fallen in; briars and hemlocks would have blotted out path, step and window; would have grown unequally but lustily over the mound, until some trespasser, losing his way, could have told only by a red-hot poker among the nettles, or a scrap of china in the hemlock, that here once someone had lived; there had been a house.

Thanks to the work and generosity of scores of individuals the melancholy fate of a deserted house, imagined by Virginia Woolf in *To the Lighthouse*, has been averted. The ethos of Charleston is preserved, at least for the time being. Now it is up to everyone who knows and loves it to ensure that it does not sink back into itself once more, this time as the embalmed object of a shallow and snobbish nostalgia concerning some 'lost and gone forever' better past, but retains its heady promise of a richer and more civilized future.

Simon Watney
1987

Chapter 1

A House for Sale

The story starts with a funeral at Firle church in May 1978. As the vicar looked round the sparse congregation, he recognized nobody. The service was short and simple. As the coffin was taken to the graveyard, Lord Gage, dressed in a dark suit, appeared at a side gate. He was paying his last respects to a man who had been his tenant for sixty-two years. The man was Duncan Grant.

He had come to Charleston, in 1916, as a young conscientious objector, to do farm work. The house and the work had been found by Vanessa Bell, who was married to, but estranged from, Clive Bell and had two young sons. She had moved out of London to Wissett Lodge in Suffolk with Duncan Grant and his lover David Garnett – also a conscientious objector – but the work there was not sufficiently arduous to count. Her sister, Virginia Woolf, had seen Charleston – a house surrounded by farmland – and had suggested they look at it. Part of the Gage family estate, it was at that time let to a Mr Stacey who wanted to sublet. They took it and moved in; subsequently renewing the lease directly with the Firle Estate. Over the years they painted almost every surface and every bit of furniture, and their pictures hung on every wall. They also created an exceptional, painterly garden. In 1961 Vanessa Bell died there; Duncan Grant lived on for another seventeen years.

Those at the funeral included: Quentin, the son of Vanessa and Clive Bell, and his wife Olivier; Angelica Garnett, the daughter of Vanessa Bell and Duncan Grant; and Paul Roche, a close friend of Duncan Grant, with his wife Clarissa. It was in the Roche's house at Aldermaston that Duncan had died. After the funeral, they all went back to Charleston, which had, in the years since Vanessa died – and even more since their faithful housekeeper Grace Higgens had retired in 1971 – fallen into a state of dilapidation.

In 1916 the house was very primitive and continued to be so for years to come. In the early months of 1918 Vanessa wrote to Roger Fry, 'This household is absolutely frozen … the cold is appalling. The only consolation is that it's so light. I sat and shivered; painting; as long as I could stand it all last week; then had a warm at the fire; then another shiver. The only thing to do is paint the mantelpieces.'

Many years later Angelica Garnett wrote:

The fascination of Charleston lies in its contradictions. The very simplicity of the house left Duncan and Vanessa free to rediscover impressions that had accumulated from things seen abroad before the 1914 war, things which may have derived an added potency from their temporary inaccessibility. The Italian Quatrocento and Romanesque wall painting can be seen behind the form and colour of Post Impressionism, but the most far reaching influence was that which came from Italian fresco via Piero della Francesca, Giotto and Veronese. It was this that enabled them to make the imaginative leap from seeing walls, doors and fireplaces as potentially tasteful background, to treating them – like canvases – as an opportunity to make a statement of a very personal nature. Such a change of perspective left William Morris and the English decorative tradition far behind and one is justifiably astonished as well as impressed by the success with which they imposed so foreign a vision on the walls of a Sussex farmhouse.

Over the years improvements had been made to the house: more running water, another bathroom with hot water, electricity, a modicum of central heating. But the house had always been damp. By May 1978, when the funeral party returned there, most of the house had been left uncleaned and largely unused for many months; but the furniture was all there; pictures hung on every wall, where the paper was peeling; piles of unframed canvases lay around; thousands of books lined the rooms. Duncan Grant's will left his pictures to Angelica Garnett and Paul Roche – the division to be overseen by Quentin Bell and the solicitor, Mungo Macfarlane. The books went to Quentin and Olivier and, apart from some specific bequests, the contents of the house to Angelica. She had previously been left all Vanessa Bell's possessions.

After her father's death Angelica lived at Charleston and tried to restore it to some sort of habitable state. During that time Michael Brundle (who was later on the Committee of the Charleston Trust and chairman of the architectural sub-committee) visited the house and, remembering it, wrote:

I first visited Charleston on an extremely cold winter's day in 1978. Virginia and Cressida Bell had provided me with a preview as to what to expect, but I was totally unprepared for the polychromatic interiors within. I had never imagined, even with their fulsome descriptions, the quality and the extent of the decorations. There seemed to be resonances from many sources mixed into an exotic brew in a lost and dilapidated Sussex farmhouse.

The effect of the forms and colour may have warmed the soul but not the body. The cold was penetrating and most of the interior surfaces seemed to be damp to the touch. It was difficult to imagine how the occupants of the house could tolerate such miserable conditions, and more depressing what on earth could be done to arrest the decay.

The siting and construction contributed to its unhappy state. The position of the house downstream to the main body of the farm and fields allows water to be directed towards the buildings. The main collection point, the pond, is located adjacent to the east façade, a coincidence that provides a picturesque prospect but excessive rising damp.

It was while Angelica was there that the pictures for the book *Omega and After* were taken by Howard Grey. The text was written by Isabelle Anscombe, who later became his wife. The designer of the book, Pauline Baines, visited the house. She remembers the penetrating cold and the feeling she was intruding into someone else's world. Everything was painted, even things whose intrinsic quality was so inferior they would not, to her, have seemed worth having.

By the middle of 1979, Angelica had decided her task was impossible and had informed the Firle Estate she wanted to terminate the lease. In the autumn of that year Deborah Gage returned to England from New York, where she had lived and worked for eight years. Although her intention was to settle in London, she felt it would be a great treat to have a weekend cottage in Firle. She had grown up in Africa and loved the open sweep of the Downs. Having just failed to secure a property which had seemed ideal, the Firle trustees told her that another one of theirs, in a similar position to the one she had lost, was for sale. She arranged to view Charleston on 28 October, the Sunday the clocks went back. Angelica had forgotten about the time change – if she had ever known about it – and was totally unprepared for this apparently very early visitor. When Debo arrived, she realized it was hardly the 'two up and down' she had in mind. But, when she had got over the shock of the overwhelming smell of rotting apples and the damp of the whole house, she began to realize that the contents and decorative scheme were unique. Although her interest was predominantly in the eighteenth century, restoring interiors of that period inevitably required a large amount of guesswork. Charleston, on the other hand, could be preserved as it really had been when its creators lived and worked there.

She went back to the trustees, to tell them the house was totally unsuitable for her personally, but she felt very strongly that it should be preserved. They suggested that she might like to undertake this; they were not interested in anything except selling the property. Not sure that her hunch was correct she rang Alan Bowness, who was soon to become Director of the Tate. He said Charleston should be saved. She then rang Richard Morphet, Keeper of the Modern Collection at the Tate, who had been a friend and associate of Duncan Grant. He gave her his whole-hearted support. Next she contacted Martin Drury at the National Trust, who said he would arrange for a team to go down and visit it. He reported back that the National Trust considered it of historic and artistic significance.

Debo reported all this to the trustees of the Firle Estate who asked her, 'What next?' She rang Martin Drury back, and he said the National Trust would consider taking it on if she could raise £720,000, which he reckoned would cover the cost of buying the house, restoring it and providing an endowment. He advised her to appoint a committee and start raising the funds.

Her next move was to ring Quentin Bell, who lived nearby in Beddingham. She did this with some trepidation, asking if he and Angelica would agree to meet her to discuss the possible preservation of Charleston. Although he had lived away from his childhood home, and away from the area, for a large part of his adult life, Quentin had always kept in close touch with Charleston and returned there frequently with his wife and children during the holidays. In 1967 he had returned permanently to Sussex when he was made Professor of Art History at Sussex University, a post he had held until 1975. In 1972 his two-volume biography of his aunt Virginia Woolf had been published and between 1977 and 1984 his wife, Anne Olivier Bell, had co-edited the Virginia Woolf diaries. No one could have been more closely associated with the Bloomsbury Group.

The meeting was arranged and she found herself in his house, Cobbe Place, sitting with Quentin, Angelica and Olivier round their scrubbed dining table sipping tea. 'Well?' he enquired, filling his pipe and stroking his beard. She replied that they needed a committee, a press release and a leaflet so that they could start raising the money to save the house. Could he help? He told her to come back the next day. When she did he handed her a folded sheet of paper containing three paragraphs.

A press release was sent out; a notice appeared in *The Times*, and many other newspapers wrote articles about the appeal. A Committee was created which consisted of Quentin and Olivier Bell, Angelica Garnett and Deborah Gage, soon to be joined by Nigel Nicolson, Piers St Aubyn as honorary treasurer, Alan Martin, and Peter Miall representing the National Trust. The trustees of the Firle Estate gave her one year to raise the money. Their patience was farsighted and generous.

Although Alan Bowness and Richard Morphet had been enthusiastic about preserving Charleston, others were not so confident it was either a possible or a sensible project. One correspondent wrote:

> I do not think the attempt to perpetuate a vanished society is often a good idea. The rooms in question usually look terribly forlorn. In the case of Charleston the 'totality'... included an air of dirt, decay and improvidence which it would be very difficult to reproduce. In fact I really should prefer to see the more conspicuous decorations taken out and put in a museum.

Nigel Nicolson had many reservations about the wisdom of trying to raise the money and of the methods proposed. He did, nevertheless, become a member of the Committee and remained so for many years. A few people approached expressed regret at not being able to support the project; Rank Xerox on the other hand sent £500, as did Harveys, the brewers from Lewes. Cheques for £1,000 were also

CHARLESTON

At first sight it is no more than an attractive farmhouse situated in a very beautiful part of the Sussex Downs. But for many decades it was occupied by artists and writers; here, Vanessa and Clive Bell, Duncan Grant, Maynard Keynes, Leonard and Virginia Woolf, David Garnett, Roger Fry, Lytton Strachey and many others were established either as residents or as constant visitors. Simply as a local habitation of genius and of talent, a theatre of intellectual activity in the first part of our century it would be remarkable. But Charleston is far more than that; from the time of their arrival in 1916 Vanessa Bell and Duncan Grant, often assisted by other artists, set themselves to adorn both the house and its garden; as a result the place was steadily enriched by an accumulation of decorative achievements, and a particular style, now a part of art history, found here its finest and most characteristic efflorescence.

Sadly, it is unique. Changes in fashion and the accidents of war have destroyed all other important examples of the domestic work of Vanessa Bell and Duncan Grant; it is only at Charleston that this chapter of cultural history can now be properly appreciated; here only we have the essential visual evidence of a life style which is extinct. If we lose Charleston a fascinating and delightful part of history is gone for ever.

Unfortunately it looks as though we shall lose it. Duncan Grant, the last tenant, died in 1978 at the age of 93 leaving the house in a sad condition. The Gage Estate, to which the house belongs, has been helpful and generous; the National Trust has been sympathetic and has the property under consideration; but neither the Estate nor the Trust can solve our immediate difficulty, which is that we need money urgently to restore, to endow, and to arrest the deterioration of the house. We hope that it may be saved and made useful. A charitable Trust is being formed which, in addition to saving the house, hopes to turn part of it into a study centre. We appeal urgently for donations.

Cheques may be made out to the Charleston Fund and sent to:
Quentin Bell
Cobbe Place, Beddingham, Lewes

Further information may be had from:
Deborah Gage
33 Palace Gardens Terrace, London W.8

Press release written by Quentin Bell to start the fundraising campaign forthcoming from Angelica Garnett and Anthony D'Offay, who organized a special exhibition of Bloomsbury paintings.

At this time Debo, still uncertain about the possibility of the whole thing, went to New York. She was staying with her friends Pierre and Tana Matisse. Sitting, having a drink before dinner, she told them: 'I've opened my big mouth to instigate a project to save Charleston. It's a huge undertaking: the house and everything in it are in a dreadful state of decay and it's terribly damp. Unimaginable funds are needed. I'm beginning to wonder if it's possible or whether I should give up the whole idea before it's too late.'

Pierre got up from his chair, went over to one of the walls and took down a Matisse sketch.

'Here you are,' he said. 'Sell this.'

She looked at him: 'Oh God, you've made it official!'

'Yes, I have!'

It was sold at Sotheby's in New York, raising $20,000.

Although the money was beginning to come in, it was clear the house was in a serious state of dilapidation. It was therefore decided, in consultation with the National Trust, that a separate charitable trust should be formed so the house could be bought and restoration started. Once this was done and the necessary money raised for the endowment, it could be disbanded and the house handed over to the National Trust. They agreed to this and offered their help and advice, which they were to give generously. In August Debo applied to the Charity Commissioners for charitable status. When this was granted, in March 1980, and the Charleston Trust was founded, the serious task of raising the necessary money to buy and then restore the house began.

Although Debo had no previous experience of fundraising, she had worked for eight years in New York, dealing in art, and so had met a number of wealthy Americans with an interest in everything artistic. She also felt that, although the British did not seem very interested in preserving anything modern, the Americans might well be. She opened her address book and contacted all the people she thought might help. She also made arrangements with the Royal Oak Foundation, a charitable organisation dedicated to preserving the Anglo-American cultural heritage, to co-ordinate the appeal in America. This allowed donors to claim tax relief; it also acted as a 'bank' collecting donations and allowing them to gain interest until they were needed for specific purposes. In addition it provided the Trust with an extensive and invaluable mailing list in America and Canada.

On 5 June 1980, the involvement of the Matisse family was augmented. A letter from Madame Marguerite Duthuit, the daughter of Henri Matisse, said she was putting a Matisse drawing in the sale at Sotheby's in December and the proceeds were to go to the Charleston Trust. Pierre Matisse put a Giacometti drawing into

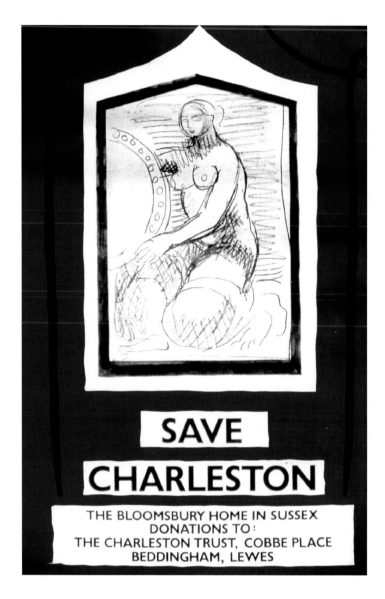

SAVE CHARLESTON

THE BLOOMSBURY HOME IN SUSSEX
DONATIONS TO:
THE CHARLESTON TRUST, COBBE PLACE
BEDDINGHAM, LEWES

The first fundraising poster, 1980

the same sale, with the proceeds to go to Charleston. Before this Debo had received £500 from the Whitbread Trust and an offer from Norah Smallwood, at the Hogarth Press, to print a brochure, with a two-colour cover designed by Angelica, and to pay £700, roughly half, towards its cost. An invitation to an Open Day at Charleston was also sent to a large number of people in the UK and the USA. This mailing and many more to come were undertaken by volunteers working round kitchen tables.

In April an exhibition of Vanessa Bell's work opened at the Davis and Long

Gallery. Richard Shone, who had often stayed with Duncan Grant in his later years and, in 1970, had painted the bath panel in the green bathroom, wrote a supportive article in the *Burlington Magazine,* of which he was the associate editor. It opened with this paragraph:

> The Museum of Modern Art, New York, recently bought a painting by Vanessa Bell of *c.*1914. To those familiar with her later work, it comes as a quite a shock to realize that she had once been in the very forefront of the avant-garde, a spirited and rebellious artist – for the painting is entirely non-representational, a dramatic collage of rectangles and spontaneous brush work … The abstract geometric impulses of this early work informs the best paintings of subsequent years. And it was put to more practical use in the many decorative schemes she undertook in collaboration with Duncan Grant. The most complete example of such decoration survives in one house only – Charleston, in Sussex, England.

However, it was the generosity of the family that really made the preservation of the house seem possible. Quentin Bell gave the manuscripts and papers connected with his biography of Virginia Woolf to Sotheby's to sell, along with a number of Woolf's personal possessions – a shawl, her glasses, her desk – which were sold on 21 July 1980 at Sotheby's, who generously waived their commission. The proceeds from the manuscripts alone brought in over £58,000.

In September 1980 a one-day symposium was put on at the Victoria and Albert Museum in London. The speakers included Nigel Nicolson, who chaired it, Quentin Bell, Michael Holroyd, Richard Morphet and Deborah Gage. It was very well attended and created a great deal of enthusiasm and publicity for the Trust. It was repeated at the Metropolitan Museum in New York the following year and similar symposia were given at the V&A in subsequent years as well as in Dallas, Texas, and Chappaqua, New York.

While in New York as an art dealer Debo had worked with Mrs Lila Acheson Wallace, the co-founder of *Reader's Digest*, who had a sizeable collection of Bloomsbury paintings and a keen interest in gardens; she had funded the restoration of Monet's garden at Giverney. Through the auspices of the art publisher, Paul Cornwall-Jones, Debo invited William Barnabas McHenry, the Wallaces' lawyer and administrator of their foundations, to come down to Charleston for lunch. On 3 September she wrote him a long, detailed letter outlining the aims of the project. It was one of a number she sent to people she hoped might support the appeal.

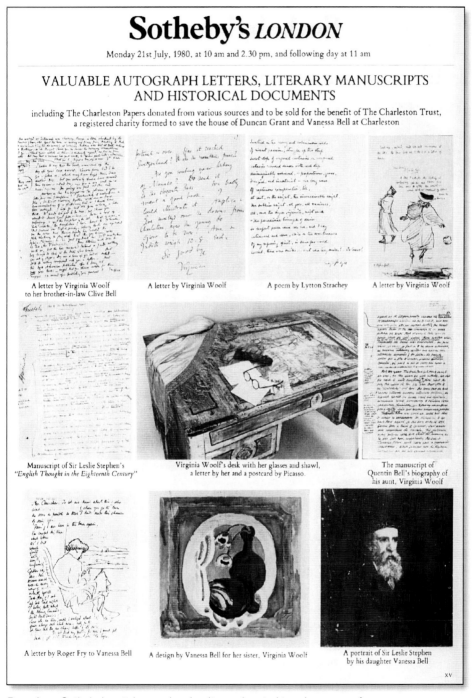

Sotheby's *LONDON*

Monday 21st July, 1980, at 10 am and 2.30 pm, and following day at 11 am

VALUABLE AUTOGRAPH LETTERS, LITERARY MANUSCRIPTS AND HISTORICAL DOCUMENTS

including The Charleston Papers donated from various sources and to be sold for the benefit of The Charleston Trust, a registered charity formed to save the house of Duncan Grant and Vanessa Bell at Charleston

A letter by Virginia Woolf to her brother-in-law Clive Bell

A letter by Virginia Woolf

A poem by Lytton Strachey

A letter by Virginia Woolf

Manuscript of Sir Leslie Stephen's *"English Thought in the Eighteenth Century"*

Virginia Woolf's desk with her glasses and shawl, a letter by her and a postcard by Picasso.

The manuscript of Quentin Bell's biography of his aunt, Virginia Woolf

A letter by Roger Fry to Vanessa Bell

A design by Vanessa Bell for her sister, Virginia Woolf

A portrait of Sir Leslie Stephen by his daughter Vanessa Bell

XV

Page from Sotheby's catalogue showing items donated to raise money for the Charleston Trust

To: William Barnabas McHenry Esq
September 3rd 1980
Dear Mr McHenry,

It was a great pleasure meeting you and your family recently at Charleston. In essence I am writing this letter wearing two caps: in the first instance, personally, as I wanted to say how greatly I enjoyed the afternoon and to express my own appreciation for your interest in the house and to spare the day to come down to Sussex.

As co-ordinator of the Appeal, I wonder whether I may also add a few lines, in order to set out some of the points discussed during your visit to Charleston.

The Charleston Trust is a registered charity in this country set up for the purpose of raising money to purchase, restore and endow the house, contents, gardens and to preserve its essential character for the benefit of future generations. Set up in this way as an independent trust allows the greatest flexibility to choose the best course for the future. The Appeal is also being directed by the Royal Oak Foundation, Inc., in New York, an American society promoting the preservation of our Anglo-American cultural heritage on both sides of the Atlantic, so that all donations made by contributors in the United States are tax-deductible. . . .

As you know we are very concerned at Charleston that the house must continue to 'live'. Whilst it is the intention to preserve the essential visual evidence at Charleston, it is also strongly felt the house *must* remain alive in order to retain its all important spirit. We hope, therefore, that while the significant rooms would be preserved and may be made available for visitors to view, those which are undecorated might serve in other ways. These parts of the house could accommodate a caretaker/curator and visiting scholar and researchers or artists with an interest in this period.

The nearby archives at Sussex University house one of the most important collections of Virginia Woolf material, all Leonard Woolf's papers, the Kingsley Martin papers and Tom Harrison's Mass Observation papers of the 1930s. Visiting scholars already use Sussex University as an important reference source; but their experience will be all the more complete if they can stay at Charleston, a house integral to that period of letters, literature, thought, social and art history and know how those who were the creative and intellectual focus of it lived.

In addition to the literary and philosophical aspects associated with those who centred themselves at Charleston, the house is essentially an artists' home. The Firle Estate have indicated further barn/s may be purchased which when converted would serve to provide extra space to allow for visiting painters – and these activities could perhaps be directed by a resident artist/caretaker. . . .

In order to achieve our objectives we require a great deal of money. Enormous interest has already been aroused in the house, and we have received overwhelming support in the press, both at home and abroad. Every major newspaper, journal and magazine has now produced features on Charleston, and I would be happy to send you clippings. In the United States we have promised the first colour article as an exclusive to the *Architectural Digest*, after which time articles will appear in other magazines and periodicals. . . .

Mrs Lila Wallace played an important role at Giverny, and we wonder whether she may be interested in Charleston, also an artists' home. I would be most grateful whether you could advise us as to how we should proceed. You have been down to see Charleston and will already have an idea of what is involved. I am sure, however, there are a number of areas which you would like to explore and go into in greater detail, and equally I feel there are specific aspects and ways in which you or Mrs Wallace would like to see a donation used.

We would most welcome your thoughts and ideas, and of course I would always be delighted to meet with you in order to fully discuss these various aspects in detail.

I shall very much look forward to hearing from you and in the meantime this comes with my very best wishes to you, and your wife and family,

Yours sincerely
DEBORAH GAGE

On 29 September he wrote her an encouraging but reserved letter. He expressed interest in assisting the restoration but wanted to see plans and costs. Specifically he was interested in seeing how the gardens might be restored and how the project as a whole would be administered after it was completed. He was in favour of using the back of the house for young artists. Debo replied to him on 6 October thanking him for his interest and promising to write again when she had more details of the work involved.

On 1 October there was a party to launch the Charleston Trust. A newspaper reported:

The £250,000 appeal to buy and repair Charleston, the Bloomsbury retreat in East Sussex, for the National Trust was opened with a drinks party given by the Marchioness of Dufferin and Ava at her house in Holland Park Villas. There a combination of Bloomsbury survivors, descendants and chroniclers suggested means of saving the house and murals, which are deteriorating fast. Speeches by Nigel Nicolson, Quentin Bell and Deborah Gage, secretary of the appeal fund, gave way to question time, when representatives of the National Trust were given a gruelling interrogation.

Amongst the Bloomsbury home team were Professor Quentin Bell and Mrs Bell, Mrs Angelica Garnett, niece of Virginia Woolf, and Stephen Keynes. Also there were Dame Peggy Ashcroft, Dame Veronica Wedgwood, Lady Bonham Carter, the Hon. Piers and Mrs St Aubyn, Sir Edward and Lady Playfair and Lady Freyberg.

Representatives from the fine arts world included Marcus Binney of *Country Life*, Alan Bowness of the Tate, John Morley and Peter Miall.

By October, thanks to the proceeds of the Sotheby auction of the Charleston papers and other items, there was sufficient confidence that enough money would be raised to buy the house and start the restoration for the Committee to appoint Pauline Plummer to oversee the interior work. Some time later she wrote:

> I little thought when I visited Charleston many years ago, as a student, that it was there I should be involved in one of the most complicated and engrossing projects of my career.
>
> My memories of that early visit are dim, but warm. I came awed at the prospect of meeting such eminent painters and was charmed by the kind manner in which I was received and put at my ease. I remember the pleasure of encountering a household of artists where every object displayed their creative enthusiasm. I was impressed by taking my lunch from original, painted plates on a unique, painted table, which I would have considered too precious to use. The studio was very cosy with sagging armchairs and limp cushions and featured a blackened stove. It was very crowded but a wonderful place to work in.
>
> I went home exclaiming, 'Everything was painted!'

Before the restoration of the inside of the house and its contents could begin, a considerable amount of structural repair was needed. The architect, Corinne Bennett of Purcell Miller Tritton, was appointed to oversee this. She was currently concerned with the restoration of the Brighton Pavilion and so was working fairly locally, and she was willing to undertake the relatively small job at Charleston. Ann Stocker was to have the day-to-day responsibility. Corinne Bennett came to the house in November 1980 and prepared a detailed report on what needed to be done to repair the structure. This report Debo showed to Mr McHenry when she met him in New York, at the end of November. By this time Angelica had moved out of Charleston and was living fairly nearby in Ringmer.

On 31 December Debo wrote an important letter to Mrs Penelope Bardel at the Metropolitan Museum in New York. Mrs Bardel was to become a significant person in the restoration and an untiring supporter in the United States. When she came to London in 1983 she became a Committee member and took on the chairmanship of the garden and grounds sub-committee, thus overseeing the restoration of the garden.

To: Mrs Penelope Bardel
December 31st 1980

Dear Mrs Bardel,

It was a very great pleasure meeting you recently in New York and may I refer to our discussion, together with Mr Richard Dougherty and Mrs S. Gautier, on December 1st concerning the aspects of a One Day Symposium at the Metropolitan Museum.

As you know, at present we are actively concerned with the restoration of Charleston Farmhouse, in Sussex, England – for more than half a century a centre of literary, intellectual and artistic activity.... The contributions of the respective members associated with the 'Bloomsbury' group who centred themselves at Charleston are varied and are constantly reassessed. The many activities we have mounted in the Untied Kingdom over the past year have met with great popularity, particularly the One Day Symposium held at the Victoria and Albert Museum in September. In view of the growing interest in Charleston being shown in the United States we are keen to mount a similar One Day Symposium in New York. We feel the Metropolitan Museum would prove the best venue, bearing in mind the links with Roger Fry and the museum. Also, the group is frequently thought of in a literary sense, and it is our desire to present their many and varied contributions in a wider sense, particularly since Charleston was the home of the artist members of the group.

We understand that the hire of the auditorium at the Museum would come to approximately $2,000 for the day and seating capacity is in the region of 700 persons. Before my departure from New York, I had a word with Arete Swartz at the Royal Oak Foundation, who suggested a date in the Fall rather than the Spring to allow ample time for organisation of the event.... The purpose of the Symposium is educational, with a view to putting forward a statement to describe and assess the contributions of the group as a whole.... Attached is the programme describing the Symposium held at the Victoria and Albert Museum, although, as we discussed, we may consider changing the format to some extent to include such speakers as Sir John Pope-Hennessy, Leon Edel and Michael Holroyd, who would provide a big 'draw' in the United States....

Yours sincerely
DEBORAH GAGE

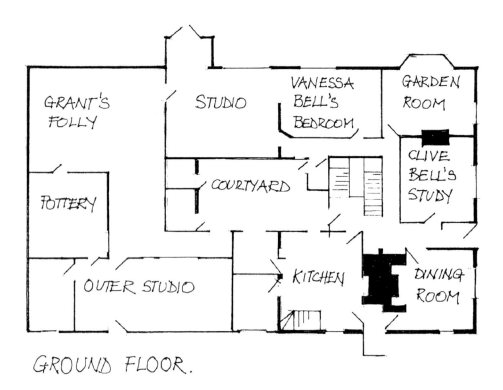

GROUND FLOOR.

Plans to show the rooms on each floor

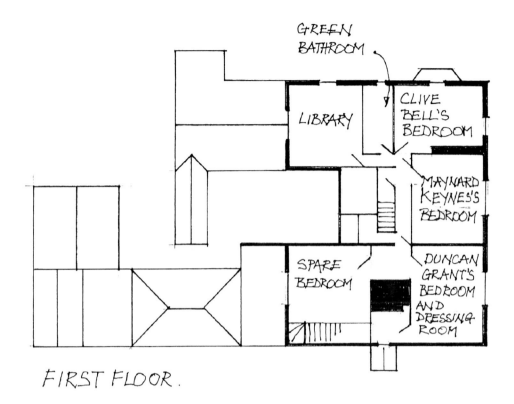

GREEN BATHROOM

LIBRARY

CLIVE BELL'S BEDROOM

MAYNARD KEYNES'S BEDROOM

SPARE BEDROOM

DUNCAN GRANT'S BEDROOM AND DRESSING ROOM

FIRST FLOOR.

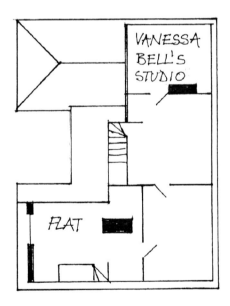

VANESSA BELL'S STUDIO

FLAT

SECOND FLOOR.

Chapter 2

Clearing the House

By February 1981 the Committee had increased in number. John Orpen became legal adviser, and other new members were Richard Shone, Peggy Post and Helen Lowenthal. On 3 February a gala performance of *Virginia*, written by Edna O'Brien, about the life and writings of Virginia and Leonard Woolf, was staged at the Aldwych Theatre, London. Maggie Smith played the lead and a special programme was produced with a wealth of sponsorship and endorsements and an introduction by Sir Hugh Casson, President of the Royal Academy of Arts and a patron of the Charleston Trust. Armand Hammer was so impressed by the evening that he promised £5,000 to the Trust to be given in ten instalments. On the same day Angelica gave a lecture in New York about her childhood at Charleston.

It was clear by March that enough funds had been raised for the purchase of the house to go ahead. Contracts were exchanged in May, but it was not until 23 June that, for £50,000, the house finally became the property of the Trust. At last its restoration could begin. Angelica Garnett generously donated the contents of the house and a number of the pictures she owned to the Trust. At the same time Vicki Walton, with her partner Cyril Reason, moved into the attic flat as caretaker/curator. They had earlier come to Charleston when Angelica, being on her own, had wanted to have other people living in the house. Cyril was an artist and used the outer studio; Vicki worked four days a week as an assistant to Quentin Bell in his pottery. She is immortalized at Charleston as the model for the fibreglass lady crafted by him, who levitates at the end of the lake. He donated it to the Trust in 1983. She not only looked after the house, but co-ordinated the work and looked after the workers with food, drink and unlimited human warmth.

The first priority was to replace the roof in order to stop water coming in, and then repair the structure of the house. Before this started a photographic archive of the rooms was made; then the home was cleared of its contents. Pauline Plummer describes what she and Joe Dawes, who was to be responsible for the architectural woodwork and the furniture, did in those early days:

Joe Dawes and I had worked together on several conservation projects combining structural and painting problems. On this occasion there were six of us. Joe brought

with him Graeme Canon to help with the checking of the furniture and the disman-
tling of the painted, architectural woodwork, while I had assistance from three Courtauld Institute students: Ruth Bubb, Amanda Paulley and Helen White. We slept in the
bedrooms and ate in the kitchen, luxuriating in the pleasure of actually being residents
at Charleston.

While Joe and Graeme carried furniture into the garden to examine and photograph
it, the paintings' conservators checked all the painted surfaces, fixing flaking or putting
on temporary facings as necessary. We found picture frames and stretchers infected
with furniture beetles. These had to be treated with insecticide using hypodermic
syringes. We knew that the paintings were to go into store and furniture beetles spread
only too easily. Two of the paintings on plywood were put aside, with the infected pieces
of furniture, to be treated later. All were marked with yellow tags saying 'gas'.

As we looked at the furniture, we soon began to realize the magnitude of the technical problems: we identified matt oil paint on chalk/size grounds over house paint;
juxtapositions of oil size colour on flat oil grounds over glossy varnish, or size colour
over oil paint on unprimed plywood; and similar unusual combinations.

All the architectural elements which could be dismantled were taken down, wrapped
in plastic and moved to the studio, while plastic was tacked over those parts which were
integral to the fabric of the house.

When the window surround in the
spare room was taken down there
was a cascade of rubble which just
missed the head of one of the conservators. One of the side panels
there, painted with a vase of flowers,
had been attacked by dry rot and had
to be saturated with a synthetic resin
hardener before storage. (Xylamon
LX hardener was used here.) Behind
the panelling in Clive Bell's study
we found both dry rot and death
watch beetle holes, so that too
needed consolidation.

A more exciting find was the dis-
covery of an earlier version of the
caryatids in the studio. When Joe
took down the oil-on-plywood

*Original caryatids, 'ruined by soot and
tarry trickles'*

versions we saw another pair, painted in size colour directly on the plaster. To our minds these were preferable, being lighter in touch and more spontaneous, but they had been ruined by soot and tarry trickles. Presumably the old Pither stove had flared up and smoked them and, being executed in size, there was no obvious way to clean them.

Joe Dawes elaborates on the problems:

The easiest items to remove were the doors and shutters, but they had been removed and refitted many times before and were hung on a variety of hinges attached with long, short, bent or broken nails and screws. All of these needed to be recorded and replaced in their original positions, as far as the breakages and losses would allow.

The fixed panels in the spare room, Duncan Grant's bedroom, Clive Bell's study, the studio and garden room were especially delicate and difficult to remove. The painted decoration was loose and flaking, which meant that any imposed vibration or bending of the panels had to be avoided, otherwise valuable paint fragments would have become detached and lost. The panels had been fixed directly to the wall, or over battens with nails and screws concealed under wood filler, before they had been painted.

An attempt was made to cut off the heads of these fastenings but this would have destroyed areas of paint. Eventually, to remove these panels with the minimum of disturbance, hacksaw blades were brazed to sheet steel strips, about 3 feet long, and moved slowly to and fro behind each panel, until the fastenings were sawn through. Whilst this was being done, the fine art conservator watched the paint surface for 'lifting', and when this happened, work stopped immediately until the paint had been reattached to the support.

In the studio this sawing could have damaged the earlier version of the caryatid and fishbowl painting.... Here gentle leverage and wedging was substituted. In other rooms a combination of both methods and the use of a metal detector helped.

In October they came back to finish packing and take down the panel in the garden room. Pauline Plummer describes this:

It was very different, the house was bare, cold and sad, the magic seemed to have disappeared and the builders were taking over. Our main task was to take down the painting above the fireplace in the garden room. It consisted of a large plywood panel with two kneeling nymphs appearing to support a framed, oval painting. It was, in fact, an oval hole, which was filled by a flower painting on plywood; behind it was a mirror which had been covered after it had accidentally been broken. The female figures were painted in size colour, the flowers were in oil. Over the three years I had been visiting the house I had noticed a damp stain gradually spreading up the right side of the panel. The size colour was powdery in places, elsewhere flakes were curled up alarmingly.

When Joe investigated the fixings of the panel he found it had been screwed from the front, before painting, through a pad of yellow strawboard, into the frame which supported the mirror.

I eased back the paint by steaming it with a kettle and then sprayed it with a thin solution of gelatine to secure the flakes before Joe started to saw behind the panel, through the thickness of the strawboard, trying to create as little vibration and stress on the plywood as possible.

The panel was taken to Pauline's studio where it could be laid flat and therefore treated with much less risk of losing flakes of paint.

Almost certainly the most challenging job was to remove and conserve the decorated wall surfaces. Indeed, there was considerable debate as to whether it was even worth trying to do so. Quentin Bell had been involved in creating one or more of them in the first place and said that he could easily reproduce a similar effect. Debo, however, felt it was vital that they should be preserved, especially as Jennifer Jenkins, of the Historic Buildings Council, had come down to inspect the house and had promised a grant of £45,000, conditional on their being preserved.

Phillip Stevens's Paper Conservation Studio was appointed to undertake this task. He later described the stages they went through:

In the spring of 1981 our first task was to carry out an inspection and prepare a report on the condition of the papers, setting out recommendations for their restoration. Plans were drawn to scale for each wall and, when the rooms had been cleared, each surface was photographed in detail and a set of large-format prints made. This would ensure that the wall surfaces on paper, which were to be removed in sections, could be replaced in exactly the same position.

It soon became evident that we were faced with a set of complex problems. The decorations had been painted in a distemper-like medium made with a base of Whiting and ground pigment mixed with a rabbit-skin glue binder in several layers and then over-stencilled or sponged with thicker layers. They tended to be insufficiently bound for the ultimate weight of paint film, which now appeared as a very brittle, dusty layer. This was further destabilized by having been painted onto poor quality, acidic wallpapers of different layers and thicknesses. In some areas in the dining room there had been no paper on the walls at all, so the design had been painted directly onto plaster, which was now in a very poor condition, due to wear and damp. In the spare room part of the paper was backed with hessian.

In all these rooms damage had been caused by abrasions from furniture, water staining, dampness, mould and general neglect, resulting in a fragile surface that, if not already flaking, could easily crack if stressed. It was decided to remove all the papers from the garden room and dining room, even where flaking and mould were extreme;

some areas would probably have to be replaced with facsimiles. Tracings were made of the design on the plaster as these too would have to be replaced. In the case of the spare bedroom it was decided to save only the architectural shapes – the marbled columns and pink arches. The large plain areas between them were very badly stained and abraded and would be best facsimiled.

While the house was cleared during the summer and autumn of 1981 we were in close liaison with Joe Dawes. The window surrounds and decorations, skirting boards and picture rails were all carefully measured, before they were taken down, to ensure their correct position when the papers were replaced. Before removing the papers we had some 'housework' to do. Surface dust and dirt, cobwebs and dead insects were taken off with soft brushes. Where the pigment was already flaking some preliminary consolidation was done using a 2% solution of methyl cellulose applied under loose flakes.

We tried using steam to remove the paper, but the paint film was so hydroscopic and fugitive that neither this nor any other aqueous method could be considered without the danger of further pigment loss. The paper would have to be cut away mechanically separating the old layers of wallpaper from the plaster behind. The width of the underlying wallpaper was ascertained (mostly 22½ inches) and sections cut to this width so that there would be no new joins when rehung.

Dining room in 1981, showing extreme areas of flaking and mould

A very effective method was devised for supporting the sections and lowering them from the walls in the rooms that had picture rails. The top 6 inches of a section were loosened below the picture rail and a thin wooden batten placed along the top edge and secured with large bulldog clips, the painted surface being protected with paper pads. Strings from either end of the batten were tied to cup hooks slotted into the picture rail so they could be pulled along.

The paper was cut away using scalpels and palette knives, working from the bottom up and from the sides to the centre of each section. Where possible the paper next to the plaster was removed; in some places there were as many as six layers and sometimes bits of plaster came away too. Each section was numbered on the back and marked on a room plan on graph paper. In areas where the paper was rotting and damp it came away very easily but temporary repairs were necessary to stop further tears or the loss of fragments. These were done with Japanese tissue and repair tape.

When a section had been fully detached it was left suspended from the wooden batten in order to dry out; each section was carefully moved back one space to allow free access to the next. The sections were left to dry naturally as any attempt to hasten this might have encouraged mould to grow. Areas of bad mould were sprayed with fungicide. When lowering a section from the walls one person released the strings while another, holding the bottom edge, guided it on to a specially constructed pallet lined

Garden room paper detached and suspended to dry

with acid-free paper. The pallets were designed to act both as support for travel and as a stacking storage system which would allow air to circulate and help further drying. They were stored at Bonhams in Lots Road in London.

Danielle Bosworth was in charge of textile restoration and first came to Charleston towards the end of the summer of 1981. She wrote:

Working with Angelica Garnett in sorting the collection helped me to understand the important part played by textiles in the household and how, once cleaned and conserved, they would again contribute to this end. Some pieces are not in themselves of great technical or artistic importance, but each has its place as a definite statement within the whole concept of Charleston.
   The collection consists mainly of:

1. Printed textiles designed by Vanessa Bell or Duncan Grant such as the curtains in the dining room and Duncan's bedroom; some pelmets; pieces used as upholstery

Garden room paper being lowered and placed on pallets

Angelica Garnett and Danielle Bosworth, who was in charge of textile restoration

material, covering chairs and armchairs; and just fragments of pieces of *The Wind* or *Apollo and Daphne*.

2. Embroidered textiles, from designs by Duncan Grant and Vanessa Bell, executed by Ethel Grant, Vanessa, Angelica and other members of the household, used as decorative panels, cushions and chair covers.

3. Commercially bought prints such as chintz curtains, squares, kerchiefs and fragments of fabrics acquired because of their pattern and colour to be used as a backdrop in a painting, to cover a cushion or simply to throw over an armchair. Some such pieces were used to cover the bare frames of lamp shades or to upholster chairs.

4. Floor coverings: rugs and rag-rugs.

5. Other textiles, such as items of costumes, lengths of cloth, table linen, acquired for their textures, to be used or worn.

Most textiles had already been listed and numbered. Our first step was to store the collection in more suitable conditions. As an alternative site was not available, low-acid cardboard boxes and acid-free tissue paper were bought. Each piece of textile was examined, thoroughly vacuumed on both sides, through a protective screening mesh, laid flat or rolled onto rollers, according to their size and shape, to fit into the boxes. Plenty of acid-free tissue paper was used to separate the layers, cover the cardboard rollers and prevent folds from becoming hard creases. The boxes and tissue paper offered protection from light and to some degree acted as a buffer against the fluctuating humidity of the environment. An added advantage in the circumstances was that they were easily moveable. The contents were checked regularly, looking for signs of dampness, insect infestation or microbiological attack. The rugs were vacuumed, rolled and covered, the chintz curtains were vacuumed and boxed, cushions were aired and vacuumed. This storage system was intended as a temporary measure until a definite storage space for the textiles not exhibited could be found.

At that stage all the ceramics in the house were simply packed away in tea chests and left until a later date to be catalogued and properly inspected. The books had been left by Duncan Grant to Quentin and many had already gone from the house. Those that were left were packed into boxes and taken to Cobbe Place.

On Saturday, 17 October, far away in the Metropolitan Museum in New York, over four hundred people attended a symposium. It was chaired by Nigel Nicolson and the programme included talks by Leon Edel, Joanne Trautmann, Richard Morphet, Sir John Pope-Hennessey, Michael Holroyd and Quentin Bell. The day ended with a showing of the film *Duncan Grant at Charleston*. It raised just under $9,000. The publicity it gave to the restoration of Charleston was immense. On 10 November, as a direct result of attending the symposium and talking to Quentin Bell and Deborah Gage, Lucia Woods Lindley wrote to Arete Swartz at the Royal Oak Foundation promising $14,000. Her later interest and support was even greater as Debo involved her closely in the work of the restoration.

Brochure for the Metorpolitan Museum Symposium, 1981

Chapter 3

Restoration Starts

While the house was being cleared, a lot of planning was going on behind the scenes. Debo, who was working unpaid to rescue Charleston, was also building up a business as an art dealer in Old Bond Street, London. She had regular architectural planning meetings there at 9.00 a.m. which were attended by Michael Brundle, Corinne Bennett and Ann Stocker. On 30 July she wrote a detailed letter to Angelica in which she gave a timetable for the work to be done during the rest of 1981. The day after, she acknowledged a donation of £2,500 from the Pilgrim Trust. Gradually the necessary funds were coming in.

Although by no means all the contents of the house had been removed they had been packed and stored in safe enough places for the structural work to start in August 1981. It was to continue both outside and inside the house until Easter 1984. The first job was to replace the leaking roof. While this was being done Vicki and Cyril were moved down to the first floor. The builders, H.F. Wilson of Alfriston, undertook all this work. The architect Corinne Bennett describes this first phase, to make the house watertight and try to cure the rising damp:

> The roofs are mainly tiled, with three lead-lined valley gutters. The kitchen porch and the roof of the bay window in the garden room are slated, the flat roof west of the kitchen is covered with asphalt and the studio roof with zinc sheets. These varied finishes were to be retained as they were part of the character of the house as the Charleston residents knew it. A temporary roof of scaffolding, corrugated iron sheeting and tarpaulins was erected over the house so that work could continue regardless of the weather and the fabric would be protected. The roofs were stripped and the structural timbers repaired and treated with insecticide. The work needed was far more extensive than could have been envisaged before the contractor opened up. The house had been poorly maintained and any repairs that had been done were of a low standard. The structure of the dormer windows on the east and south sides of the house had to be completely renewed. The main roof timbers, though generally of oak, were of no particular archaeological interest and the design was haphazard. The only unusual feature was a large 'A' frame, one leg of which was the hip rafter at the south east corner of the roof, with the other leg running down diagonally behind the large brick chimney stack

containing the kitchen and dining room flues.

The roofs were felted and battened, all the sound clay peg tiles sorted out for reuse and the numbers made up with matching second-hand tiles. The lead valleys, dormer cheeks and a small flat roof over the ground floor lavatory were re-covered with 7- to 8-lb cast lead. The brick chimneys were partially rebuilt above the roofs, incorporating lead damp-proof courses and rendered externally. During the rebuilding a sack of straw was put down each flue to prevent bricks and dirt falling into the rooms below.

The zinc covering on the studio roof was replaced with aluminium sheet, which looks similar but is more durable. The timber-framed roof-light in the north-west corner of this room was also renewed as it had almost disintegrated. Lastly, the eaves, gutters and downpipes were completely dismantled, cleaned out, repaired, painted and refixed to make sure the rainwater from the roofs was carried away.

When this work was complete the building was safe from water coming in from above and its appearance remained the same.

In order that further repairs to the structure of the building could go ahead funds had to continue to be found. By the end of 1981 just over £150,000 had been raised; an additional £1,148 was held by the Friends of Charleston on behalf of the Trust and $54,000 was held by the Royal Oak Foundation. The expenditure was just over £96,000. At this time Debo conceived the idea of asking people to sponsor individual rooms. It was yet another way of closely involving those who were willing to give money with the restoration of the house itself. She and the Committee put an estimated cost on each room which worked out as follows:

Dining room	£8,500
Garden room	£8,500
Clive Bell's study	£6,000
Studio	£10,000
Vanessa Bell's bedroom	£5,000
Kitchen	£6,000
Courtyard	£5,000
Duncan Grant's bedroom	£7,000
Spare bedroom	£7,500
Maynard Keynes' bedroom	£5,000
Clive Bell's Bedroom	£5,000
Library	£6,500
TOTAL	£80,000

In addition they estimated costs for other places:

Curator's flat	£27,000
Visitors' amenities	£21,000
TOTAL	£48,000

Vanessa Bell's studio	£5,500
Studio/attic space	£7,500
Garden	£25,000
TOTAL	£38,000

The first three people Debo wrote to were those who had already given or pledged large sums. They were Pierre Matisse – his sister Marguerite had very recently died – Armand Hammer and Lucia Woods Lindley. She wanted to give them first pick and sent them descriptions of all the rooms and offered to send photographs. She also said their sponsorship would be commemorated. There was some discussion as to how this should be done; but eventually it was decided their names would be put at the top of the room description in the guidebook. The Giacometti drawing had made £2,100 and the Matisse sketch £6,500 in the Sotheby's sale, a total of £8,600. Armand Hammer had donated £5,000 and Lucia Woods Lindley had pledged $14,000 but had raised it to $15,000, roughly the equivalent of £8,000. Pierre Matisse chose the dining room, Armand Hammer Maynard Keynes's bedroom and Lucia Woods Lindley, after some deliberation, the studio, increasing her donation to £10,000. Debo wrote to Pierre Matisse: 'We are all delighted that you have chosen the dining room at Charleston and I understand you wish it to be commemorated as follows:

Marguerite Duthuit, her son Claude and Pierre Matisse
in memory of Georges Duthuit'

Later other rooms were adopted. The Robert Huffins, Jr Foundation chose the kitchen, the T.V.S. Trust Duncan Grant's bedroom, the Eugene McDermott Foundation the garden room, and the Henry Jackman Foundation Vanessa Bell's bedroom. Mary Jackman originally wrote to Debo asking whether the restoration by the National Trust of Virginia Woolf's Monks House was complete and went on to be a keen supporter of Charleston. At this time, and for some time to come, the plan was to hand the property over to the National Trust once the restoration was complete, so the link with Monks House was obvious.

On 16 June 1981 the first Annual General Meeting of the Friends of Charleston took place and the emptied house was opened. Remnants of the contents were still there and photographs showed what it had and, hopefully, would look like. Diana Reich was one of a considerable number to come to the Open Day and later wrote about it. Her article ended:

Vanessa Bell's two living children, Professor Quentin Bell and his sister, Angelica Garnett, are now vigorously involved in trying to donate part of their background to the public. They are active and informative emblems of a lost epoch and, for the sake of posterity, are prepared to tolerate the invasion of intimate images of the past by groups of 'Friends'. If they succeed in helping to preserve Charleston they will have accomplished something more than embalming their own childhood and commemorating a group which has become part of literary and cultural mythology. As well as supplying an irreplaceable visual record Charleston is a tribute to a way of life which incorporates certain values and beliefs which are worth memorializing and contemplating. I suspect that Charleston represents something different for each of its new 'Friends'. My Charleston is an engagingly un-grand house, in lovely surroundings, which contains a collection of beautiful and imaginative creations; but, above all, it was the house and meeting place of a group of people whose progressive, intellectual, artistic and social attitudes embraced the vision to perceive that responsibility and risk need not be incompatible.... For a charmed afternoon, last June, Charleston was once more resonant with animated discussion and effervescent laughter. Suddenly it did not seem too daring to hope that the house and its contents could be permanently protected and that the Trust would be able to establish a residence for visiting artists, writers or academics in part of the building, so that Charleston, and what it embodies, might not be allowed to vanish forever.

By 1983 Diana was a Committee member and publicity manager for the Trust. She has since become a pivotal person in the whole organization as Artistic Director of the hugely successful Charleston Festival, which takes place every summer. She is also Artistic Director of Small Wonder, the only short-story festival in Britain, which is held at Charleston in the autumn. Hugh Lee had been recruited to the Committee in 1981 to look after the Friends and edit the Newsletter, which was to keep the Friends and others aware of what was going on during and after the restoration.

Members of the architectural team were at the Open Day and answered the many questions that were put to them. By June the next phase of the structural work was well underway, as Corinne Bennett describes:

The second phase of the work was less straightforward and included strengthening the floors. As a start the floorboards and the ceilings below them were removed from the second floor joists and a few non-load-bearing partitions were taken down. Much of the floorboarding had been heavily attacked by beetle, both furniture beetle and death watch, and had been repaired by fixing new boards on top of existing ones, with inevitable reinfestation. The structural timbers were of oak – 8 inch by 8 inch main joists carrying 4½ inch by 4½ inch secondary joists – tenonned into the main members.

For some reason, perhaps connected with the original timber-framed construction of the house, the main beams were spanning the longer dimension in each room, with subsequent sagging, especially where the ends of some of the beams had rotted at the bearing in the wall. As we did not wish to alter the finished appearance of the floors or ceilings in any way, we had only the depth of the secondary joists – that is 4½ inches – in which to strengthen the floor. The amount of steel used was kept to a minimum as too much additional weight would have been self-defeating.

While this work was in progress the electrical wiring for both the first and the second floors was installed as well as the pipe runs for the top floor radiators, new bathroom fittings and the water storage tanks. The ceiling below the roof, including the sloping areas, (or 'skeelings' as they are called locally) was completely renewed and insulated with glass fibre.

Plate designed and made by Quentin Bell to celebrate the centenary of Virginia Woolf's birth

The centenary of Virginia Woolf's birth fell in 1982. To celebrate it Quentin Bell designed and made a hundred plates which were numbered on the reverse, signed by him and carried the Fulham Pottery mark. They were offered for sale at £95 each to raise money for the Trust. In the announcement of this offer Kenneth Clark wrote:

> Fifty years ago I commissioned a set of plates by Duncan Grant and Vanessa Bell. Recently they were on exhibition at the Victoria and Albert Museum in London. These plates have always been a source of pleasure to me, and I now warmly commend this work, commemorating the centenary of Virginia Woolf's birth, produced by Quentin Bell, nephew and biographer of Virginia Woolf and son of Vanessa Bell.

They were displayed by Christie's in London and New York and, by the end of the following year, most had been sold, many to American buyers. Interest in Charleston had always been greater in America than England and in October 1982 American *Vogue* carried a long article by Mary Blume about the history of the house and the progress of the restoration. It was largely an interview with Quentin Bell, conducted as they walked through the house a year earlier.

Chapter 4

More Repairs More Money

As well as extensive work on the house, 1983 was the year of the raffles. Amazing prizes were donated by a number of companies and people. They included exotic holidays and free air travel, and the artist John Ward offered to paint a portrait. This was won by Jane Dunn, author of *Virginia Woolf and Vanessa Bell: A Very Close Conspiracy*. She later wrote:

> He likes to say he won me but the truth is I won him. Only third prize in the Friends of Charleston Raffle … but he was the only prize I wanted. Life isn't usually so accommodating, but this once my name was drawn; the privilege of having my portrait painted by John Ward RA, painter of poets, princes, society beauties, presidents and captains of industry was mine.

After a vivid description of the sitting she ends:

> I have been invited back to sit in that cool silence and be painted again. I make time to go – it is a thoroughly inappropriate and extravagant reward for a raffle ticket that cost a mere 50p. Thank you, Friends of Charleston.

John Ward had written to Debo saying he thought he had offered to do a drawing not a painting and the most he could do was a watercolour portrait. When he saw who had won he clearly changed his mind.

A showing of *To the Lighthouse* in New York in April, introduced by Nigel Nicolson,

Jane Dunn won the prize of having her portrait painted by John Ward in a raffle

with American champagne donated by a Californian vineyard, was more of a publicity success than a financial one; but as the majority of the money had come, and did come, from America this was well worth doing. It was at this showing that the result of another raffle was announced. The first prize was two return transatlantic air tickets; other prizes included Quentin Bell commemorative plates. In all the raffles raised £7,980.

The next phase of the structural work on the house was no less challenging than the earlier ones. It is described by Corinne Bennett, H.F. Wilson and Nick Hunt, the young plasterer, who had worked exclusively in the traditional manner on timber-framed buildings:

> The third phase consisted of repairing the floors on the ground and first floors; renewing much of the plaster on the walls and ceilings and repairing the windows and doors. The floors on the first floor were of similar construction to the ones on the second so the repair and treatment of the structural timbers and boarding did not present any major new problems. The floors in some of the ground-floor rooms were of suspended timber construction but only the ones over the cellar – that is in the corridor leading to Vanessa Bell's bedroom – needed strengthening. The supporting timbers had been attacked by beetle so were treated with insecticide and a small amount of steelwork was added in the cellar.

East-facing window showing rot and water damage

The floor in the dining room had a screed covering old porous tiles and this was taken up and replaced by a ventilated, suspended timber floor. The kitchen floor was also taken up, a concrete slab laid and covered with second-hand quarry tiles which came from a firm in St Pancras, London. It was impossible to find enough tiles of the same size to cover this large area so two different sizes were used. This was a challenge to the bricklayer because a 'tight' joint was required; a wide joint, which is used today, makes it easier to lose irregularities.

The timber partitions that were of lath and plaster were in a very poor condition and had to be stripped down and new treated laths fixed, covered in haired lime plaster. This trade went out when plasterboard came into use. The importance of using these traditional plaster mixes is that, unlike modern plaster, they allow the walls behind to 'breathe' and, if necessary, water can evaporate steadily through the plaster and walls without damaging them.

Before the existing plaster could be removed the shapes and contours of the walls had to be recorded for the refitting of the decorations. To achieve this hardboard templates were scribed horizontally and vertically every 3 feet on each wall. These were used when replastering in order to give an exact copy of the original walls. Once the old plaster had been removed and necessary remedial work to the timber and brickwork had been carried out, replastering could begin.

Tanalised sawn wooden laths were fixed with galvanised nails to the timbers of the internal stud work. A gap of approximately ⅜ inch (traditionally done by placing the end of the thumb between the laths) was left between each lath to form a key for the plaster. The plaster was made up of: lime putty, which had to be brought from Wales; sand, which was a washed sharp-mixed aggregate obtained locally (the mixed aggregate gives better building properties); and long goats' hair to give tensile strength and bonding.

The first mix used – known as 'coarse stuff' – consists of three parts sand to one part lime putty, goats' hair, which has to be beaten into the mix and uniformly distributed, and water. This is then applied to the walls and ceilings to give a keying coat. It has to be applied in the same direction so the 'squeeze' behind the laths is the same.

When the laths have been evenly covered the surface is scratched to form a key for the second, floating coat. This is traditionally done by sharpening four laths to a point, nailing them into a fan shape, 2 inches apart, then scoring the wet surface with a diamond pattern.

When the first coat is dry, which can take up to four weeks, the floating coat can be applied. This is the same mix as the keying coat and is applied in the normal way. At this point the hardboard templates were used as rules to re-create the irregularities of each wall. When this was achieved the floating coat was devilled to form a key for the finish coat. This was done by scoring the surface with nails protruding ¹⁄₁₆ inch through a float. When this has dried, which can take up to eight weeks, the setting or finish coat can be applied. This is called the 'fine stuff' and is made up of one part lime putty to two parts

North-facing wall stripped back to the timber framing during repair work

clean silver sand with enough water to make a creamy consistency. It is applied in three thin coats and finished with a wetted, cross-grained wood float to avoid shrink-crazing.

During the replastering evidence of the timber-framed construction of the house came to light. In Maynard Keynes's bedroom an inner lining had been built about 8 inches in front of the south wall. This was so badly decayed that it had to be taken down and the original wall behind it revealed the timber framing. Even more dramatic was the framing exposed on the north wall of the house. Here the external rendering was in such poor condition that it was decided to remove and totally renew it, rather than try to patch it. When the rendering was removed the oak-framing was found, although considerably altered by the addition of the bay in the garden room and the insertion of a large window when the studio was created on the top floor. Essential repairs were made with new oak and then the framing disappeared once more behind new rendering, but not before a drawing had been made.

A lot of thought was given to the method of heating the house, as its precious contents and the structure itself could be affected by it. At first it was proposed not to use central heating in the ground-floor rooms but to have portable oil-filled radiators, which could be used in the winter and removed in the summer. Eventually it was decided to have an oil-fired boiler in the cellar, with radiators in each room, to give a gentle background heat in the house, which had never been properly heated before. Traditional cast-iron, column radiators were used; they were discreetly placed, often close to or behind doors, or partially concealed by the panelling, as in the dining room. A great deal of trouble was taken to conceal the pipework. In the kitchen the old black-leaded cast-iron range, set in the chimney alcove, had long been disused and an Aga had been put in front of it. Both the range and the Aga were removed and replaced with a second-hand oil-fired Aga, to warm the kitchen and for cooking.

Finally, a lead drain was laid around the south, east and west sides of the house to try to prevent water from the farm above running below the foundations. This was not entirely successful as there were almost certainly hidden springs under the house. From the Ordnance Survey map it can be seen that most of the old farms and houses nearby are on much the same contour as Charleston, which would suggest they were situated with care on the spring line below the Downs, to provide water nearby. Later other measures had to be taken to lessen the danger of rising damp, which was making it impossible to replace the decorated wall surfaces.

On 2 December 1983, Debo wrote a long and detailed letter to Mrs Norman Hickman, the Chairman of the Royal Oak Foundation, whom she had recently talked to in New York. The foundation was pivotal to the success of the campaign in America and the support of Mrs Hickman and her successor Susan Weber Soros was invaluable. The main subject of her letter was the American committee, which had originally included a number of distinguished and influential people, including Henry

Geldzahler, Mark Lancaster, Mitchell Leaska, Robert Tobin and William Lieberman. For a number of reasons they had stepped down and when Arete Swartz moved to North Carolina and Penny Bardel to London the whole committee seemed to have fallen apart. Arete Swartz had been the Director of the Royal Oak Foundation and was succeeded first by Arthur Prager and then Damaris Horan. Debo listed a large number of possible committee members and contacts who might help in raising more funds in America. An informal committee was soon formed which included Robert Tobin, William Lieberman, Susan Komarow and Amanda Mecke. By the end of the year the total funds raised had reached £308,917 which was a little more than the goal stipulated by an anonymous American donor to trigger an additional sum of £50,000. This donor was Mrs Lila Acheson Wallace.

On 3 December Debo wrote to William Barnabas McHenry to say that the structural repairs to the house were almost complete. Referring to his offer, on behalf of Mrs Wallace, to sponsor the garden and grounds, she suggested they should meet when he was going to be in London over Christmas. She went on:

> In Duncan Grant's later years the garden was simplified, borders put down to grass etc. What we would like to do is to re-establish these borders; then there will be further work repairing the flint wall and re-establishing the statuary which ran around its top. Penny Bardel … has recently moved to London and now heads our 'garden committee'. She is presently drawing up and costing these plans and ideas.

He enthusiastically agreed to meet them both and confirmed Lila Wallace's interest in the restoration of the garden. He also stipulated that they would like Sir Peter Shepheard to research its original design and draw up plans for its restoration, and suggested that he meet with them as well. On 6 February 1984 he wrote expressing his delight they had agreed that Peter Shepheard should work on the garden, and said that he would ask him to start preliminary research in the spring and that they would pay all the development costs.

Coincidentally, Peter Shepheard, as a young man, had been accepted into Professor Charles Reilly's prestigious department at Liverpool School of Architecture. In 1936, he obtained a first-class degree, and won the graduate scholarship – open to the whole university – with his civic design project. The scholarship demanded a year's research; his was into the history of gardens. It was Professor Charles Reilly who involved Duncan Grant, Vanessa and Quentin Bell in the decoration of Berwick Church.

Chapter 5

Dallas and Decoration

In July 1983 Debo wrote to Mrs Pat Porter to discuss in further detail plans for a symposium, similar to the one at the Metropolitan Museum in New York, to be held either at the Meadows School of the Arts at the Southern Methodist University in Dallas, Texas, or at the new Dallas Museum, whose Director, Harry Parker, had been at the Metropolitan Museum in New York. It was also to be supported by the Kimbell Museum in Fort Worth and was to coincide with a literary festival and an exhibition of *The Bloomsbury Artists: Duncan Grant, Vanessa Bell and Their Friends*, hosted by Irene Martin of the Meadows Museum and Patricia Porter of the Southern Methodist University. There was considerable correspondence about this during the first half of 1984 including asking the Duke and Duchess of Devonshire if they would be willing to lend some of their paintings and attend the symposium. They agreed to both requests, and the symposium was planned for Saturday 27 October.

The run-up to Dallas provided evidence that Debo's search for sponsorship was not always easy. She was turned down by American and Caledonian Airlines when she asked for free flights for the participants; and she had a memorable letter from an old friend which said:

> It was a pleasant surprise to see your characteristic handwriting after so long – this time in your request about 'The Charleston Trust'. To be truthful, there is no group you could have picked less sympathetic to me than the Bloomsbury lot. If this farmhouse had no connection with those people I might have been capable of a mild, slight concern for its future.

However, the support she received far outweighed the refusals.

Mrs Lila Wallace died in June and it was decided to dedicate the symposium to her. It was introduced by William Lieberman of the Metropolitan Museum and chaired by Nigel Nicolson. The speakers were Margaret Drabble, Michael Holroyd, Angelica Garnett and Richard Shone, with concluding remarks by Nigel Nicolson. There was also a showing of the film *Duncan Grant at Charleston*. It attracted a large audience and was greeted with great enthusiasm. Like the one at the Metropolitan Museum, it resulted in a considerable donation, this time from Mrs Margaret

McDermott. She had long been a supporter and friend of Debo's and later increased her donation to £8,500 to sponsor the garden room. During 1984 just over £111,000 were raised, most of which came from America.

As well as praise it also gave rise to a newspaper report:

Departed from the city are two leading members of British aristocracy, the Duke of Devonshire, whose Chatsworth family estate contains hundreds of framed art works, and the Marchioness of Dufferin and Ava, who is an artist and spent the mornings here at her Plaza of the Americas hotel room sketching. The Duke was in Dallas as a lender of five Bloomsbury group paintings, a circle that by British standards of the 1920s and 30s was considered more than slightly risqué. The legends behind the paintings gave a freer than usual spirit to the preview exhibition last Friday at SMU. Among those lending paintings for the exhibit was Queen Mother Elizabeth. The group was in Dallas to raise support for the Bloomsbury's commune-salon known as the Charleston House, which is part of the British National Trust.

Clearly it's not only the British press that gets things slightly wrong.

By the time this was being written considerable progress had been made back at Charleston. While the structural work was being carried out a lot of consultation had gone on between Debo, the rest of the Committee and some of the conservators about how each room should be 'restored'. Over the years almost every room had been used for a variety of purposes. It was finally decided to put the house back to about 1939, when Clive Bell moved down to live there. The exception was the Maynard Keynes bedroom. He had ceased to use this room when he married in 1925, but, as he was such a pivotal figure in the early days of Charleston, it was decided the room he had used would be remembered as his. There were also a number of decorative changes made after this date – most notably the decorated wall surfaces in the garden room. In

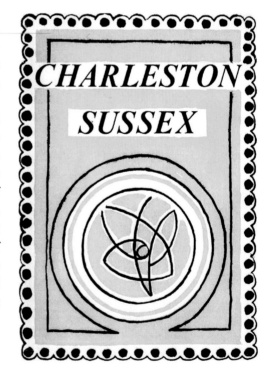

Cover of fundraising brochure designed by Angelica Garnett

February 1984, a memorandum drawn up by Nigel Nicolson and amended by Debo and Quentin Bell, mentioned the 1930s date amongst many other things. It looked forward to the probability of opening to the public at the end of 1985 or in 1986. It postponed the provision of lodgings and studios for visiting scholars, and limited the endowment to the National Trust to a maximum of £200,000.

In October 1984 a beautifully designed fundraising brochure was produced by the Hogarth Press as their contribution towards the Charleston Appeal. It had a yellow and black cover design by Angelica Garnett, contributions by Deborah Gage, Quentin Bell and Richard Morphet and was illustrated with four black and white photographs. On the back it listed the many distinguished patrons. It still assumed that the house would be handed over to the National Trust, although the endowment they were asking for exceeded, by £540,000, the one fixed as the maximum by the Committee earlier in the year. This assumption was eventually abandoned.

In the first half of 1984 two exhibitions in London, at the Crafts Council and the Anthony d'Offay Gallery, gave unprecedented publicity to the Omega Workshops and so to Bloomsbury and particularly to Charleston. By Easter Vicki and Cyril were able to stop moving from room to room and were back in the attic, in a greatly improved flat. They also had the use of the kitchen, which had been modernized. At last the job of decorating the house and conserving its contents could begin in earnest.

Probably all conservators receive criticism from laymen; Debo certainly did. One of the Committee members questioned why the walls had to be left to dry for so long, quoting his builder as saying four days, or at most two weeks, was enough. He had surely not recognized the difference between modern plastering with plasterboard and the far more complicated method that had been used at Charleston; nor had he taken into account the nature of the paper to be applied to the walls once they were dry. Other questions concerned the apparent loss of time, forgetting that funds were not unlimited and many of the things to be treated were stored at Charleston – where there was no safe space to work – and could not easily be moved without damaging them.

The only things that had been treated were the linen chest in Maynard Keynes's bedroom, which was sent to the Crafts Council Exhibition in London, the door from Clive Bell's study and the caryatid surround from the studio, which were prepared for an exhibition in Brighton of *Treasures from Sussex Houses*. Pauline Plummer wrote:

> The acrobat door was covered with layers of brittle house paint before it was first decorated and these had to be fixed. An ugly gash in the lower panel was filled and retouched, while blanching on some parts of the painting made it necessary to use surface coating of different strengths in different areas. When things were sent to exhibitions it was often necessary to do more retouching than would normally be used for those left in the house.

The first work on the interior of the house was undertaken by a firm called ELLE, which comprised two ladies called Elaine Ogilvie and Cindy Watts. They were a local firm and a newspaper article about them said: 'Their experience covers almost every type of home, from manor house to farm; town house to bed-sit. No home is too small and no two jobs are the same.' Charleston was certainly very different from anything they had done before. Their job initially was to 'distress' the walls and mix paints in the right colours. They described the challenge:

The walls had been repaired with goats' hair plaster but some of the original was still intact. Unfortunately, quite a number of stains had bled through the plaster. Several views were expressed as to how to deal with these. Eventually it was decided to brush the stains with shellac; then stick small Japanese paper pieces over the stains ending with a further brushing with shellac. The Japanese paper had to be torn roughly to fit the shape of the stains, some of which were quite large. We were worried at first how we could cover these patches but in fact they worked to our advantage because all the new walls were to be 'distressed'. This involved making the new walls look very old.

Acrobat door panel after conservation

Various things were done to achieve this. On both walls and ceilings we put layer upon layer of special acid-free lining paper, making sure we overlapped edges and put as many creases in the paper as possible. A major problem was that the paper was originally to have been delivered from London as one roll, which was approximately equivalent to 300 rolls of normal wallpaper! Eventually it was delivered in the equivalent of twenty normal rolls. Each roll was still incredibly heavy so we rigged up a device with a broom handle supported on two fire extinguishers, which made it easy to unroll.

We had to distress all the new woodwork – skirtings and door frames, where necessary. This involved bashing the skirtings with hammers or planing chips out. In the hallways and landings we made the walls have a very uneven surface by building up lumps and bumps with modern-day Artex, then brushing or distressing it to make it look 'lived-in' and old. In the studio we had to overcome the problem of making the roof ceiling area look wishy-washy and old. We were able to balance planks across the beams and used oil-based flat paint – similar to old-fashioned distemper.

One of the differences by 1984 was the involvement of the family. While the structural work was going on it had been overseen by Michael Brundle and none of the family members had felt it necessary to be involved. Debo had, however, come down to Sussex most weekends and would sit round the scrubbed table at Cobbe Place, and later in Heighton Street, talking for hours to Quentin and Olivier and sometimes Angelica if she was around. She was very aware of how the conservation of their house was impacting on the family, and was concerned that things should be done with their approval. Once the detailed decorating started things changed. In a letter to Debo on Christmas Eve 1983 Quentin said: 'There will be three of us who have seen Charleston at various points in its development. Our task will be expensive in time and energy but not I hope in other ways.'

The ELLE ladies continue:

The paints used were interesting in that they were very different from the gloss and emulsion used today. The idea was to use what would have been used in the Charleston era. Restorers came down to mix the colours using 'ingredients' such as rabbit-skin glue, size and powder colours. We would spend on occasion hours making up paints to match the existing colours; these would be approved by various members of the family and then in would walk the restorers and throw up their hands in horror, exclaiming the colours were definitely not right. We would stand in the background while a decision or compromise was made. This could often take two or three days. At one point Angelica Garnett came back from France [she had gone to live in the South of France in July 1983] to mix paint ready to go on our recently distressed walls. However, she found the whole project and being at Charleston – from what we understood –

depressing and so returned to France leaving buckets and buckets of paint made up in the 'right' colours. We were then asked if we would mind applying the paints – this was not originally part of our job but we said we would. Unfortunately that type of paint goes off fairly rapidly and so within a couple of weeks we were opening buckets of rancid paint one after another. They had all gone off and so had to be remixed.

While Angelica was there in March 1985, she mixed large quantities of paint. She was somewhat demanding, and every time Debo arrived at Charleston she was told to go back to London to collect yet another pigment from Cornelissen. Angelica decorated Duncan Grant's bedroom, the library and the green bathroom. She remembered being told that the library walls were originally covered with green patterned wallpaper, which had given a special effect to the black paint. She managed to reproduce this by mixing a little yellow with the black, leaving the paint 'streaky' and then brushing the surface with a broom. She also repainted the walls of the dining room black.

It was while she was there that Wilma Harper, a member of Pauline Plummer's team, joined the painters. She takes up the story:

In March 1985, when Angelica Garnett arrived from France and began mixing paint for all the non-patterned rooms, I took up when she left off; her time was limited and it was

Angelica painting the dining room walls

imperative to apply the distemper as soon as possible (even with the addition of a biocide this medium only keeps for a short while). I remember asking Angelica *how* she painted as I felt it was important to familiarize myself with her style. Whether it was my phrasing or my Irish accent her answer was, 'Up and down with a brush!' Despite this helpful tip I found her brushstrokes more defined and the colour more boldly worked than I could naturally achieve myself. However, I decided that, particularly with distemper, an individual hand would be more consistent in matching specific colours than trying to copy Angelica's. Indeed in Duncan Grant's bedroom a light wash of whitish distemper and a little spraying was thought necessary to soften the finish. It was felt Angelica's brushstrokes were rather pronounced and too 'fresh' looking.

Where possible the final colours were matched to original samples – remains of painted paper or surviving paint fragments. Photographs were also used but these were of limited use as the colour reproduction was unreliable. Matching the spontaneous style of the Charleston artists and achieving a sense of harmony and balance appropriate for the house was, of course, more difficult. Although thorough research and accurate colour matching greatly helped, the final results were achieved more by feel and sympathy than lengthy technical groundwork and cold-blooded application.

Paint was always mixed in the morning as the light at Charleston changes so dramatically during the day. The mixes and their proportions were always noted and tested in various parts of the room, either on walls – which could easily be washed again – or on pieces of paper. These were then looked at again the following morning before a final decision was made. In order to maintain a consistent, accurate match and a fluid approach samples were usually mixed in 2 gallon batches. The sieving and mixing was a time-consuming process, and running out would have meant starting all over again. Such large quantities of paint clearly presented storage problems and the endless covered containers could be found everywhere, although mostly in the fridge along with the team's lunch. My industrious sessions at Charleston were always remarkable for the curious 'festering feet-flavoured fodder'!

In Vanessa Bell's bedroom it was unanimously decided to paper over the remaining original paint – with the exception of the air-vent – as the extensive staining would have made restoration impossible. The original decoration of the walls was achieved in two separate washes – pink followed by grey. Those who had an intimate knowledge of the house expressed different memories: some felt it was predominantly grey and others predominantly pink. It was then found that two different mixes of paint had been used for the original pink wash: on the wall facing the garden it contained the pigment Alizarin, which gave it a stronger more purple-pink hue; on the air-vent on the opposite wall, as well as in some fragments, there was none of this pigment. Also this wall would probably have seemed greyer as it got less light. Those parts of the walls which had sustained most wear and tear may well have had some of the grey wash worn away, making them look pinker.

With such conflicting information it was hardly surprising that the first attempt at redecoration proved unsatisfactory. The walls were washed down and re-sized and it was generally agreed that the final result, based on the colour found on the air-vent, gave a generally accurate overall effect. The paint mixes, using Cornelissen's artists' pigments were as follows: pink – Venetian Red, Red Lead, Yellow Ochre, Whiting; grey – Ivory Black, Raw Umber, Indian Red, Whiting. The pigment Alizarin does not mix well in distemper and so was not used.

Angelica had already mixed two colours for Clive Bell's study but by the time it came to put them on the size had gone off and the smell was awful. It was so bad that everyone coming into the house by the front door had to hold their noses. The green for above the fireplace and picture rail and the yellow for the walls worked well together but the yellow bore no resemblance to a description of the original – like 'faded wrapping paper' – and neither colour related to any available photographs or appeared to be 'Charlestonian'. During the remixing great care was taken to match as near as possible to the original. As there was only very limited information this was not easy and further frustration was experienced in trying to make the two colours work together as well as Angelica's had. Both these aims were significant factors in attempting to achieve a true 'Charlestonian' effect.

Clive Bell's study with paint pots. Duncan Grant's granddaughter Nerissa painted the room green and yellow in 1971

In the end a satisfactory balance between the two was found. With minor adjustments a similar base to Angelica's yellow was eventually used. The green was more difficult but by chance some evidence of the original was found on the fireplace and on a discarded picture rail. These fragments amounted in total to about ¼ square inch! Six months later Phillip Stevens found he had a small piece of the original green paper amongst various wallpaper samples he had taken some while before. It was a great relief to find that the final colours we used were after all quite accurate. The paint mixes using Cornelissen's artists' pigments were: yellow – Yellow Ochre, Venetian Red, Whiting; green – Medium Chrome, Lemon Yellow, Chrome Oxide, Yellow Ochre, Raw Umber.

Although great care was taken to reproduce the yellow and green in Clive Bell's study, it was known that these colours were not there in 1939. Many years later, in 1971, they were mixed, under Duncan Grant's direction, by Nerissa, his granddaughter, and the room painted by her. It was thought interesting, however, to show how the decorative scheme in the rooms evolved and changed over the years.

Maynard Keynes's bedroom was much easier but in order to give it additional texture it was given two applications, the second one being slightly thicker. It was also given a certain amount of distressing to age it. The mix used here, again using Cornelissen's artists' pigments, was: off white – Ivory Black, Whiting.

In the spare room the underlying colour had been yellow under the decorative arch and column effect. Once the plain pink panels which form the arches and the stippled columns had been restored and reattached the yellow ground followed by a lilac-grey wash were painted inside the arches. Any of the original yellow peeping through where it was not wanted was sprayed out. From photographs it was apparent that the yellow only showed around the edges of the arches and in occasional places where the top layer had rubbed off. Quentin Bell was always at hand to emphasize that there should be no straight lines so great care was taken to ensure the grey and yellow edges were as free as possible. The mixes, again using Cornelissen's artists' pigments were: yellow – Yellow Ochre, Medium Chrome, Viridian, Whiting; lilac-grey – Indian Red, Ivory Black, Whiting.

The room that was known as the 'infamous' blue loo had been painted many times over the years, and much of the paint had begun to flake off. After removing some of the later layers a blue was found that could be dated to the 1930s. The walls were rubbed down, sized and repainted to match this colour. The mix of Cornelissen's artists' pigments was: blue – Cerulean Blue, (a little) Raw Umber, Whiting. Brodie and Middleton's decorator's pigment Cerulean Blue was also used as the artists' one is very expensive.

All the ceilings in the rooms were painted with Craig and Rose oil distemper coloured with stainers, mostly Raw Umber and Ochre. This proved much more time consuming than had been anticipated, particularly in the spare room, as the different light in each room meant a slightly different mix was needed. The ceilings and walls in the corridors, hall and stairway still had much of the original distemper. Any new plaster was touched in with matching distemper.

The obvious space to use as a workshop to repair and conserve the furniture that had been stored was the studio; but it required a considerable amount of work itself. It had already had parts rebuilt and reroofed, and the ceiling and roof area had been painted. Pauline Plummer describes what also had to be done:

The studio provided a large number of interesting problems. I have already described the finding of the earlier version of the caryatids. When it came to treating them they were flaking badly and a solution of Klucel G (hydroxypropyl cellulose) in acetone was flooded gently over the loose flakes, which were then rolled back into place with swabs soaked in acetone. Some of the flakes – about 1½ inches long – were floating, completely detached, on the ends of long strands of cobwebs. These were captured on soft, sable brushes and coaxed back into their correct positions. Once the paint had been secured, I started to work over the soot-covered upper parts and found it was possible to improve the appearance of the painting considerably using solvents and mild abrasives. After cleaning, further consolidation was done with gelatine. There was no retouching as the paintings were to be covered up again and in any case large areas of the modelling in the centre of the figures was missing and one would not retouch without more evidence of what had been there. It is a principle of the conservator's ethic that there must be no falsification of the artist's intentions.

The over-mantel which consists of two still-lifes flanking a simulated niche was also painted in size colour and had suffered from water seeping down through the chimney stack. After fixing first with Klucet G and then with gelatine, small losses were toned in with pastels.

The end wall of the studio had been painted buff with a blue border and had subsequently been given a thin wash of black applied with random brush strokes, all done with size colour. This wall had been replastered so I carried out a large-scale re-creation of the colour and texture with pigments bound in gelatine which I attempted to age with scratches and dribbles and small retouchings, so that it would blend in with the original colour on the adjoining wall. Latex masking fluid gave some excellent effects here.

The opposite wall, painted in grey and aubergine, had suffered from a leaking roof and was striped with trickles from ceiling to floor. Katherine Stainer-Hutchins performed marvels toning in these streaks with size colour and a spray gun to reduce them but not obliterate them completely. They too had been a part of the décor for a long time, as had the spots of paint all over the floor.

Chapter 6

Conservation of Furniture and Wooden Panels

Geraldine Guest had been attracted to the work of the Charleston artists in the 1970s by Simon Watney's description of their work and more recently, in early 1984, by the Omega Workshops exhibition at the Crafts Council. Her interest led her to become a Friend of Charleston and she had been to Open Days and attended various seminars. She wrote to Vicki and Debo telling them she was a conservator of ceramics and asking why nothing was being done to the considerable number of these in the house. They replied immediately telling her there were no funds to undertake this at the moment but they had not been forgotten. They invited her to come to the house to meet Pauline Plummer and examine the collection.

On arrival at Charleston I found myself captivated by its peace and tranquillity broken intermittently by the team of restorers at work on the decorated surfaces and furniture. I knew then that I was witnessing a remarkable and unique project in which I very much wanted to be involved…. At this point it was suggested by Pauline that, until more funds were available to proceed with the work on the ceramics, I could join her team working on the decorative surfaces on the furniture and the rooms. I readily agreed and started work touching in the flaking grey paint on the doors and the skirtings in the corridors.

For this I used artists' acrylic paints, mixing them to the varying shades of grey with water and where appropriate a small amount of fumed silica matting agent to reduce the shine. To test that my colour matching was exact – as acrylics dry approximately four shades darker – I accelerated the drying time with a hand-held dryer. In areas where the original paintwork was too dirty or dull I cleaned it carefully with a very mild solution of sugar soap in warm water taking care to rinse thoroughly to avoid streaking. It was then allowed to dry and where necessary a solution of one to ten microcrystalline wax and white spirit was applied with a cotton-wool pad, using a circular motion and buffed up immediately, to restore it to a matt finish.

Where small areas of door, mouldings, window shutters or skirtings were missing a two-part epoxy wood putty was used, which could be moulded and carved down to the appropriate shape. For shallow areas that did not occur on an 'edge' fine-surface Poly-filla was used. This was then painted in the same way as before. It had been decided to retain finger marks, paint splashes and patina. Where new woodwork had been added because the original was beyond restoration, it was necessary to prime, colour match and then distress using Raw Umber etc. Pauline and her team were always at hand to give advice and whilst they were still there I worked on the fireplace, skirtings, door surrounds and window embrasure in Duncan Grant's bedroom, 'marbling-in' pipes and light switches in the spare room and colour matching and painting-in areas below the paper collage in Clive Bell's bedroom.

The largest piece of painted furniture in the house was undoubtedly the bookcase in the library. This had been built for Clive Bell's library in Gordon Square and decorated for him by Duncan Grant. When Clive moved down to Charleston in 1939 the bookcase came with him. In 1970, six years after Clive's death, Duncan Grant wanted more space to hang pictures; so the bookcase was taken down and moved to Cobbe Place, along with the books. The wall behind it was in a bad state, probably caused by damp from the bathroom next door. When Quentin and Olivier moved from Cobbe Place to Heighton Street in 1984 the bookcase came back to Charleston. As a result of all this moving there was quite a lot of structural and superficial damage.

The library bookcase, originally built for Clive Bell's library in Gordon Square and decorated for him by Duncan Grant

It was clear that when it first came to Charleston a hammer had been used to bang it into place to the left of the door. This damage was left. Geraldine Guest took on its restoration during the winter of 1985, when most of the other people had gone away. She wrote:

> This was by far the most challenging and rewarding job. After the carpenter had repaired the structure it had to be cleaned, filled and touched-in, using the same techniques as on the rest of the decorated furniture, taking care not to make it look overly restored. When cleaning the skirting of the bookcase I discovered, hidden under the more recent white emulsion, an Indian Red stripe continuing right round the bottom, which suddenly gave sense and proportion to the rest of the decoration. This stripe was then completely exposed and touched-in.

The white emulsion on the skirting can be seen in the photograph, taken for the book *Omega and After* in 1979, when the bookcase was at Cobbe Place.

Another notable piece of furniture was the dining table. Pauline Plummer describes its treatment:

> The circular dining table occupied several conservators at one time. The top is of laminated pine with two drop leaves. It proved to have been painted in size colour and given a heat-proof varnish. When cleaning we found a thick coating of dirty wax polish, which once removed took with it many of the signs of domestic use. It then became apparent that there was an earlier design showing faintly through the paint. It was known that Vanessa Bell had redecorated the table [the earlier version is evident in the picture of *Helen Anrep in the Dining Room* by Duncan Grant which hangs in Maynard Keynes's bedroom]. Next we found there was a cushion of wax between the two paint layers, which made cleaning a great deal more difficult, as one feared to lose any of the top layer.
>
> In the positions where the residents had sat most often, the painting was completely worn away, exposing the bare wood. I decided to complete the ground colour in the bare areas and to continue the lines of the upper design slightly over the edges of the losses but not to retouch it completely. I wanted it to be obvious how the paint had worn away over the years but without leaving the dark tone of the wood to distract the eye from appreciating the design. I left the shadowy shapes of the earlier version showing through the later one, so they were not immediately noticeable but, once observed, provided enough information to allow one to reconstruct the pattern in one's mind. This super-imposition must have been visible for some long time and is very typical of Charleston and the way themes were reworked over long periods. Retouching was done with Rowney's Cryla paints and the table was given a thin, picture varnish on the assumption that it would not be subjected to heavy use in the future.

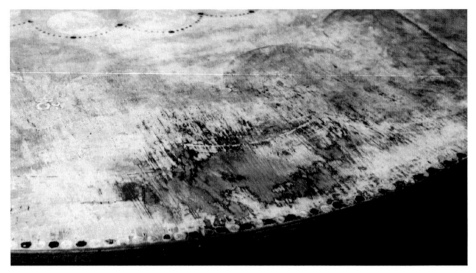

Dining room table before, with the paint completely worn away

A lot of the rest of the furniture was treated by Joe Dawes in his workshop, along with a number of the wooden panels. He describes the aims and processes:

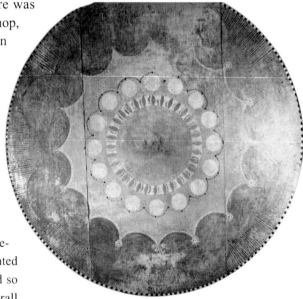

Dining room table after

Within the house there is a very wide quality of joinery and a catholic range of loose furniture with pieces from England, Italy and France. Various periods, styles and qualities are represented ranging from good antiques to inexpensive 'white-wood' items, which had been painted in the Omega Workshop style and so were very important to the overall decorative scheme. Furniture conservation tries to stop ageing. This is the objective of the average museum. However, unlike a museum, some of the furniture at Charleston will still be used, as visitors tend to ignore the request 'not to touch' and lean on tables and sit on chairs. It was therefore decided that repairs should be the minimum to ensure the article was safe to use. This obviously excluded visible metal plates, brackets and screws.

The first thing was to clean away the dust and dirt left by storage and a decade of neglect. This was largely done by volunteers, using water mixed with a little white spirit, vinegar and detergent, applied and wiped dry quickly to reduce the 'wetted time', which would lift the grain of the wood and create rough patches.

The joints in furniture, especially chairs, are subject to considerable stress. So the adhesive used must be strong and also compatible with the residues of old glue remaining in the pores of the wood after cleaning. The hot animal or 'scotch glue' is compatible and, if things go wrong, easily reversible with heat and water. Because broken joints tend to have become excessively loose over the years they have to be built up with new wood veneers on the tenons before rejointing.

Veneers are the visible surface of the furniture and when refixing with hot animal glue there are two problems: first, wetting, which would make them expand and become too large; and second, getting the temperature wrong, which could destroy residues of original polish and patina on the surface of the veneer. To avoid both of these the veneers are lifted, propped and quickly cleaned with a steam jet from a kettle fitted with a tube and a nozzle. This softens the old glue and makes it easy to scrape away. Then the 'ground' is coated with hot scotch glue which is left to gel; the veneer is put down; the glue is remelted with a hot caul or sand under pressure until the joint has 'grabbed'.

Many of the linings or internal framing of carcases were disintegrating from woodworm or wear and tear from drawers. These were repaired or replaced using as much of the original wood as possible. Previous DIY repairs were dismantled and assorted PVA, rubber and modern-type adhesives stripped off and replaced with traditional glues. Some new parts had to be made to replace completely destroyed or missing parts, which, after grafting-on, were colour tinted with alkali if possible, otherwise with oil, spirit or water dyes depending on the finish required.

All the furniture was given a final coat of wax. On dark coloured woods the scratches and minor damage tend to show white. This was toned down by using a heavy pastetype wax coloured brown for oak and walnut and reddish for mahogany. This wax is a grain filler and is rubbed across the grain, left for a time – neither too long nor too short – and then rubbed down with coarse hessian or a shoe brush. For furniture with a gloss finish nitro-cellulose or French polish is best because it is a much lighter wax. Small pinholes and defects were filled with dyed beeswax applied with body heat; larger dents were in-filled with pigment dyed Beaumontage, made from equal amounts of beeswax and resin.

Traditional cabinetmakers' techniques were used to replace brass inlays and loose fittings: scotch glue with a little plaster of Paris and Venice turpentine added. Blackened brass handles were cleaned with a rotary bristle brush. The objective was to avoid an over-polished look and retain the used, comfortable and worn appearance of the furniture's metalwork.

In all over a hundred pieces of furniture needed repair – these varied from replacing a loose castor to refixing 220 pieces of veneer and the embossed five-piece leather inset on the writing flap of Vanessa Bell's desk.

The refitting of the painted panels, after they had been conserved, posed very different problems. They could not be attached in the same way as they had been originally. Joe Dawes explains:

It would have been unwise, given the fragile nature of the painted surfaces, to use nails or screws. Also the panels needed to be removable to give access to the plumbing and the structure of the building, and to allow for possible future conservation. Invisible mountings were needed. For the thinnest ones, in Duncan Grant's bedroom, where there was no space behind the panels, Velcro fabric fasteners and spots of panel mounting adhesive were used. The green bathroom panel and the garden room panels were mounted on double frames of sweet chestnut wood – a stiff, durable wood with good sliding properties which looks much like oak. The first frame was fixed in position with stainless steel screws; the second, identical frame was fitted with keyhole screws and fitted over the first; the painted panel was then bonded onto it with neoprene adhesive. Sliding the panel to left or right releases the screw head which allows it to be lifted away.

In the spare bedroom, knuckle jointed battens had to be made and angled exactly to the wall profile and the shape of the reveals. In the studio the caryatid painted panels were attached with concealed hinges, so they could be opened to show the earlier wall paintings. In Clive Bell's study, stainless steel pegs and plates were attached to the window panels and to the wall, with stainless steel screws making them, like those in the green bathroom and garden room, removable, while looking exactly the same as they did before.

Joe Dawes, who treated much of the furniture, in his workroom

Chapter 7

Fabrics –
Conserved and Copied

Once the structural work had been completed it was possible to unwrap the textiles. Danielle Bosworth was in charge of them and she describes the procedures:

It was decided that remedial conservation should proceed in order of priority. Textiles which were designed or executed by members of the household or occupied an important place in the interior were to be treated first. Each of these was photographed and its size, construction, materials and decorative elements recorded – including thread counts and spinning and plying directions. At Charleston the textiles were very much

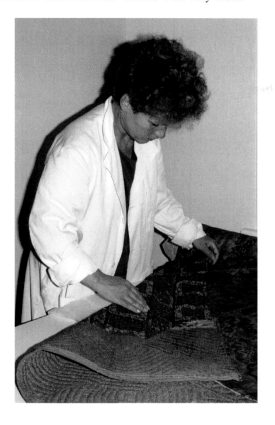

used and their condition was poor. It was obvious that for many years no steps had been taken to prevent their deterioration.

The first thing to be treated was the embroidered panel of flowers and butterflies that hung in the studio. The canvas was unevenly nailed to a stretcher and surrounded by a very plain wooden frame. It had no backing or glass and was resting close to a wall. In spite of all this, the linen canvas structure was still strong; but both surfaces of the embroidery were dusty and dirty and the wool had many broken ends and a few missing stitches, which gave it a rough appearance.

Danielle Bosworth, described by Diana Reich as 'being able to transform most rags into riches'

Looking at it under a magnifying glass showed that the type of soiling was twofold: surface grease held dust on the raised fibres and a black coloration seemed to have become ingrained in the fibres. As there was a solid-fuel stove in the room, it was assumed that molecules of carbon may have chemically cross-linked with the degraded wool fibres as well as making them dirty. This type of chemically bonded soiling is difficult to remove without using chemicals incompatible with weak protein fibres and dyes.

When the embroidery had been released from its frame, it was assessed for wet cleaning and the wool yarn was tested for fastness. It was considered strong enough to withstand washing, provided the surface was treated very gently to avoid damaging it. The panel was thoroughly vacuumed on both sides, through a protective screen, and then laid on a length of nylon to give it support during the washing. It was immersed in a washing solution with a pH of 6.2 at 20°C and soaked to allow the fibres to swell and release dirt. When dirt began to be released after twenty minutes, the solution was changed. The pH was raised to 6.8 during four successive washes. It was gently sponged on both sides, with more emphasis on the back, until no more dirt appeared. A small amount of dye was released during washing. After numerous rinses in soft and then deionized water, to remove all traces of detergent, the last rinse was acidified to a pH of 5 to 'fix' the tan colour, which in tests had shown a tendency to bleed, but responded favourably to acetic acid. Rust stains on the surrounding canvas were not treated.

After draining the last bath, the panel was lifted out of the washing tray, using the net support, and laid on a pad made of clean white absorbent cloths with another similar pad laid evenly on top. A board and weights were placed on the sandwiched panel to extract as much moisture as possible. It was then laid face down on a polythene covered board and pinned out to dry. This was to ensure that no movement occurred during the drying process and that the face of the embroidery would be smooth. Drying was accelerated to minimize the risk of dye migration. When it was dry the loose stitches were secured and the whole panel was given a boiled cotton support, attached with a running stitch of fine cotton-covered polyester thread, sewn in both directions to form a grid. It was then mounted onto a stretcher, glazed and dust-proofed, with a piece of lining cloth fixed to the back of the frame.

Four canvas embroidered chair seats were the next to be treated. They were badly upholstered and only a few nails held the embroideries to the framework. They were very dirty and stained and one of the embroideries had a large transversal tear, caused by use and the badly padded seat. However their general condition was strong. After they had been released from the frames they were vacuumed and the colour fastness tested.

Because they were so badly discoloured it was decided to try to release some of the ingrained dirt, which would clearly not be removed by simply washing. After a pattern of the shape and size of each seat cover had been taken the dirtiest was immersed in white spirit (BS254) for eight hours and then washed in the same way as the embroidered panel. The dirt had largely gone but the staining remained. The pH was raised to 8 by adding tri-sodium phosphate which also acted as a sequestrant, increasing the cleaning power of the solution. It is not normally advisable to use tri-sodium phosphate to wash dyed wool, as it is too harsh for protein fibres and dyes, but in this case it was worthwhile to remove as much of the staining as possible. The remaining three seat covers were treated in the same way.

Each piece was then dried pinned face down onto a polythene sheet stretched over the previously traced paper patterns to ensure the shape and size of each would fit the seat of the chair. When they were dry they were stitched onto boiled linen fabric in both directions to form a grid. Any repairs to the embroidery were made through the linen.

Most of the curtains in the house were home made. The ones in Duncan Grant's bedroom were made of warp face eight-point satin: the finer, warp threads were spun from rayon (regenerated cellulose), the coarser, waft threads were cotton. They had been machine stitched with very small stitches. The print had faded a great deal and seemed generally dull. They were very dusty, although they had been cleaned a few years before. The design was further obscured by large brown stains which occur when very degraded cellulose has got wet and then been allowed to dry. The brown degraded material migrates by capillary attraction and is deposited in a 'tide-line' on the edge of a dry area. In the brown stained areas the warps were very weak or had disintegrated totally. The damage was greater where the curtains had been handled.

The brass rings were removed, the hems and side seams unpicked and the curtains thoroughly vacuumed. The print was tested for colour fastness. After they were given temporary support the curtains were washed and laid face down to dry. Glass slides and weights were used to hold the edges and prevent wrinkling. The broken threads were neatly aligned according to the grain and care was taken not to stretch or break the rayon fibres, which are normally more plastic and less strong when wet. Washing was successful in that it gave the fabric back its shine, but sadly the brown stains remained, although they were less dark.

A fine cream dyed cotton fabric was scoured and then used as a support to the weak and broken areas, taking care to align the grains. The loose weft threads were carefully straightened and stitched with a very fine polyester thread in a 'couching' technique. The edges of the patches were also stitched down to keep them flat.

When these curtains were originally made the lengths of cloth were cut following neither the design nor the grain. It was felt in the remaking that a compromise should be made to make the print look as straight as possible. The top hems were strengthened with washed cotton tape and the curtains were relined with washed cotton lining material. The original brass rings were cleaned and re-stitched through the linings and cotton tape ready to be hung.

These examples serve to illustrate how, although general conservation rules were applied, we were conscious that the textiles were very much a part of everyday life at

Charleston. I understood from Angelica that household chores were dealt with in the morning and the afternoons were spent on creative work. This included covering cushions, running up curtains and canvas embroidery as well as creating designs for printing and other things. The freedom of expression seen in the prints can also be found in the execution of the embroidery. Duncan Grant supplied most of the designs in the form of small sketches and was frequently consulted by those who were carrying them out. Decisions on how to keep to the design or suit the feeling of the sketch were taken jointly. The creative process seems to have been all important and this element of creativity must be carried through to present day Charleston.

Danielle Bosworth was described by Diana Reich as 'being able to transform most rags into riches', but there were many pieces that even she could not conserve. The Committee members were faced with a dilemma: should some of the fabric designs be allowed to die or was it possible to find a fabric manufacturer to reproduce them, and, was this a good idea? They were influenced by the success of the two recent exhibitions, which had brought the work of the Omega Workshops to the attention of the public and served to highlight Duncan and Vanessa's pioneering work in the decorative arts. This led them to decide that they should not only explore the possibility of reproducing the fabrics required for Charleston, but also investigate whether they could be reproduced and sold for profit.

It was Allan Walton who had originally contacted Duncan Grant and Vanessa Bell, in 1931, with the suggestion that they should design fabrics for him. This meant, for the first time, their designs were available to more people than the friends and relatives who had given them commissions. However, even then, the fabrics only sold through several sophisticated shops and galleries so, once more, the artists had relied mainly on personal contacts. In the Second World War Allan Walton's business had closed down. But the fact they had once been commercially produced made it easier to decide it might be possible again. Diana Reich was given the job of approaching fabric manufacturers. She takes up the story:

Fortunately one of those serendipitous events, frequently associated with the restoration of Charleston occurred. Nick Ashley, the son of Laura Ashley, had developed an interest in the Omega Workshops and in the art of Duncan and Vanessa in particular. He was immediately responsive both to the idea of replacing the fabrics which were specifically required at Charleston and to giving some of Duncan and Vanessa's designs a new lease of life in his commercial collection. He offered to provide the fabrics for the house as a donation to Charleston and to buy the copyright of the designs to be produced commercially.

It was obviously critical to have the commitment of the family members; had they not supported the idea it would not have been worth pursuing at all. However, they took the view that Duncan and Vanessa were flexible and empirical people who would have regarded it as a challenge to comply with modern production techniques and the demands of a new clientele. As we knew that minor adaptations to the original prints would be necessary it made sense to give Angelica Garnett, who was intimately familiar with her parents' artistic intentions, the last word as to whether a particular design was sufficiently compatible with the original to be ready for production.

Laura Ashley only re-created one Omega fabric, White. The softer Allan Walton fabrics seemed more suited to the ambience of Charleston and more in keeping with the rest of Laura Ashley's collection. A very clear distinction was made between the fabrics which were re-created especially for Charleston and those which entered the Laura Ashley commercial range. The colours and some details of the design were not to be the same. The guiding principle for the Charleston fabrics – Grapes, Grapes Border, West Wind, White, Duncan's Urn and Abstract – was that they should correspond as closely as was reasonably practicable, in terms of material, colour, scale of repeat and graphics, to the original form.

The original West Wind fabric

Nick Ashley elaborated on this:

The fabrics for Charleston had to be as near as possible a replica of those designed and printed in the 1930s, and it was not only the designs which had to be reproduced but the fabrics themselves. One of our main problems proved to be colour accuracy. In order to ascertain the true colours originally used we first unstitched the lining and hems of curtains or removed fabric from upholstered furniture in an attempt to find protected slivers of cloth. These tiny preserved bits were remarkably bright and vibrant in contrast to the faded colours of the sections exposed to light and dirt. Rather than reproduce the fabrics in their original colours it was thought best to find a shade halfway between the two, as this would sit better in the now softened colours in the house. When it came to choosing the colours the old piece of fabric was stretched out on the table and scrutinised to find the tiny patch that was the exact shade of brown, pink, red etc. A pin was then stuck into this patch and the whole thing sent off to the colour laboratory. Bruce Wright, our in-house colour authority, then had the task of finding the exact dye and tone mixes.

As this was going on our cloth buyer, Peter Brown, was trying to source cloths – by no means an easy task. Most of the fabrics were rough linens or cottons and were fairly easy to find once the exact construction had been established. The one that posed the real problem was the slub rayon which had been used for West Wind and Duncan's Urn. Slub was an irregularity of cloth which gave it a richer texture. Rayon cloth was a new development in the 1920s and 30s, and, just as nylon stockings became the fashionable alternative to silk ones, so rayon was the 'trendy' new fabric for the home. However, as Quentin Bell pointed out, the reason why Duncan Grant and Vanessa Bell probably chose to print their designs on rayon was that it was cheap and available from the local shop. Natural fibres have since come back into fashion so an exact replica of the man-made cloth that was so readily available in the 1920s and 30s, was impossible to find. We did manage to track down a slub rayon which was a 90% match.

Various dyes react in different ways to various cloths and, as all the colours to be used in the re-creation of the Charleston fabrics were totally different from any used in the Laura Ashley palette, it meant starting the whole process from scratch. Exhaustive tests were carried out as we could not predict how cloth and dye would react to one another.

Another problem we encountered was the size of the pattern repeat used for some of the designs. Fabrics such as West Wind have a pattern repeat of 120 cm and the roller system we use to print Laura Ashley fabrics has a maximum repeat of 91.4 cm. This meant researching an alternative form of printing. To reproduce these designs to the quality required meant having them printed with a flatbed technique, which allows for a larger repeat pattern.

At this time, as Diana describes, there was a great deal of communication back and forth with Angelica Garnett, who was by then living in the South of France.

Lines were frequently hot between London and the Alpes-Maritimes and we all became adept at long-distance descriptions of minute shifts in shades and slubs. Angelica would inspect strikes sent through the post or by special courier, usually one of Laura Ashley's design team, and give her verdict. On one notorious occasion the fabrics and the courier were impounded by French customs; the designs obviously possessed a certain explosive *je ne sais quoi*!

Nick Ashley finishes the story:

When the cloth and dye recipes had been found and the printing technique for each design sorted out we trial printed each design by hand, to check the accuracy of colour and design, before printing the larger quantities required for the house. I was very nervous about showing these to Angelica Garnett and the other members of the Committee, who came along to see and discuss the results of everyone's labours. But my fears were groundless. All parties were very pleased and excited and few changes had to be made.

Chapter 8

Stained Glass

If the famous stained-glass artist Alan Younger had not visited Charleston during one of the early Open Days, it is quite possible that Quentin's stained-glass panel would never have been replaced in the door of Maynard Keynes's bedroom. This would have been a pity, as it is yet another example of the diverse interests and skills of the group. While walking round the garden and house, Alan Younger was introduced to Angelica Garnett and talked to her about his work with stained glass. She took him up to the 'out of bounds' area on the first floor of the house and showed him the panel, which was standing against a wall. She explained that it had originally been made by Quentin in the 1930s and was one of two which had been installed in the side windows of the porch which, at the time, was outside the front door. When this was later taken down Quentin moved one of them to the door of what was then his bedroom. At some time, much later, it had fallen out of the door. It was badly damaged and several pieces of glass were missing.

Alan Younger tells what happened next:

My offer to restore the panel was accepted and we discussed whether it should be carried out as a surprise for Quentin Bell. Later I decided it would be more prudent to show him the restoration in progress and ask his advice about colours for the missing bits. Before driving back to London with the glass packed in my car and, incidentally, forgetting to leave an address, so that Angelica Garnett must have wondered if she would ever see the glass again, I made a template of the opening in the door where the glass would be refitted.

Inspecting the panel in my studio, I discovered approximately one-third of the glass was missing and a few pieces were broken. What did remain was barely held in the leads, due to several years of door vibration, and some pieces had probably been cut rather too slack to fit fully into the leads. Also the cement which weatherproofs stained glass and holds the glass securely in place was now crumbling and falling out. Possibly, judging from its colour, a substitute recipe had been used at the time the panel was made.

All the leadwork was in a poor state but fortunately was intact and completely indicated the original layout of the design. It was necessary to re-lead the whole panel with

new leads; this meant the whole thing had to be dismantled and any cement still cling-
ing to the glass removed. In order to do this and preserve a record of the design a full-
size rubbing, similar to a brass rubbing, was made. The template of the opening taken
at Charleston was set out on linen cloth, forming a rectangle. This was laid over the
panel and an impression of the leads made by rubbing cobbler's heelball over the surface. Two different widths of lead had been used and these were recorded.

The exact position and shape of each piece of glass was established, including the
missing shapes indicated by the leadwork. It was then safe to release all the glass pieces
and discard the old lead. The glass was cleaned and placed in order on the rubbing.
Some adjustment was made to compensate for the original slackness in the cutting and
a strong pencil mark was made around each piece to form a new cutline. No special pre-
cautions had to be taken to clean the glass, just water and a stiff brush, as none of it had
been painted with enamel and there was no surface deterioration.

The invention in the nineteenth century of Norman slab glass, much favoured by the
Arts and Crafts Movement, encouraged artists to use less paint and rely more on the
intrinsic quality of the material to give a rich and glowing effect. Quentin Bell's panel
was entirely made from Norman slabs and all the pieces left unpainted.

The panel was made at Charleston, where Quentin Bell found glass left over from
the time when Vanessa Bell had been producing stained glass work for the Omega
Workshops. A few extra slabs were bought from the main supplier, James Hetley and
Company, who were then in Soho Square; the remainder came from Surslem, where
Gordon Forsyth was Principal. It was his enthusiasm for stained glass that first aroused
Quentin Bell's interest. The main excitement was technical and the Charleston panel
was made just after a visit to Canterbury and was his third attempt to work in that
'fascinating but difficult medium'.

The design might be described as loosely symmetrical and it was therefore possible
to work out from the existing colour layout the pieces, mainly blues, rubies, opalescent
whites and various browns, that were missing. A symbol for these colours was marked
on the outline in preparation for cutting the new glass.

The manufacture of Norman slab glass had ceased in the early 1960s and finding
suitable glass of this type proved very difficult. Amongst scraps tucked away in my
studio I found sufficient blues. Several telephone calls and visits to look through stocks
of old glass rarely produced Norman slabs and never the right colours. Coming to the
end of my list of possible sources I called on Moira Forsyth, then in her last year at the
Glass House in Fulham. She had designed and made windows there since 1935 and
still had in her racks some glass from before the war. She was extremely pleased to let
me have pieces when we discovered exactly the right tones of colour and texture. It
was most appropriate and a very happy coincidence that Moira, daughter of Gordon
Forsyth, who had originally inspired Quentin Bell to make stained glass, should supply
some of the replacement pieces fifty years later.

Having solved this problem I was able to cut the new pieces to shape. These and all the other glass were then temporarily stuck in position with plasticine onto a large sheet of clear glass. Imitation lead lines were painted on the reverse side with black paint so that the complete panel could be judged up against the light before being glazed into the leads. Using this method it was easy to make any necessary changes. I moved a few pieces to distribute the original glass more evenly. One of the new large blue pieces in the centre lacked texture and I had some doubt as to how deep the tone should be. I slumped three slabs, of different tones, in my kiln to produce more character and provide a choice. These I took, with the 'mock-up' panel to Cobbe Place, where Quentin Bell was living, so that he could see all the glass before it was leaded. We propped the panel up in a window and tried the various blues, eventually selecting the deepest tone. We decided all the other colours were satisfactory.

New leads were made to the original widths and the panel was glazed in my studio using the outline to position the glass accurately. Each lead joint was soldered on the back and front. Finally it was cemented and laid horizontally to set for a few days before cleaning and polishing with sawdust. The complete panel was returned to Charleston in June 1984 ready to be reinstalled in the door.

Chapter 9

Ceramics

When Geraldine Guest was finally able to unpack the ceramics, which had been put away in tea chests, they covered the whole floor of the spare room. Nothing had been done to them, and some were clearly in need of immediate attention. The rest were divided into categories and stored away, some in cupboards and others in shelving added for the purpose. Geraldine Guest describes what she found:

> The majority of the collection is heavy-bodied earthenware, mostly tin-glazed (faience and majolica) chargers and vases. There are examples of creamware, marbleware, spongeware and some Staffordshire figures; also parts of two Chinese export porcelain dinner services with blue and white and green and white decoration. It is a varied and interesting collection, spreading across the nineteenth and early twentieth centuries, acquired by inheritance, during time spent abroad in Europe and the East or produced by the artists themselves, the family, their friends, and at the Omega Workshops.

Because it was obviously undesirable for the house to be devoid of all ceramics when it was opened, it was decided to display a number of pieces which were only slightly damaged, or had been repaired with rivets or dowels. These she dusted and cleaned with a mild solution of detergent and warm water using swabs of cotton wool. The metal rivets or dowels she similarly cleaned with white spirit. Once these had been treated she selected other pieces that were obviously or extensively damaged, but relatively stable, and wrapped them to take back to her studio for further examination and assessment. She then began work on the pieces that had been earmarked for immediate attention, because of their extremely delicate state. She describes what she did to three of these:

> In the set of glazed terracotta tiles, decorated with an abstract design by Duncan Grant, five of the six tiles were broken into at least four pieces and their edges were very worn down in places through rubbing together. They were still in an old wooden frame, forming a tray, which sat in front of the stove in the studio. The shards were surrounded by and covered with ash, grit and dust from the stove. In some areas, along the breaks, this had begun to penetrate the body of the tiles. The main problem was how well the

edges would clean and then fit back together again. There was no old restoration and the glaze was not flaking at all, so, after carefully sliding them out of the frame and removing candle wax with a scalpel, I washed them in detergent and warm water. Because of a low firing temperature the body of earthenware or terracotta is left porous, so, before bleaching the edges of the shards, they had to be soaked again in clean water so that the bleach did not penetrate too far, pushing the stain into the body. When they had been soaked I mixed a solution of enzyme washing powder and water softener – 2% – in warm water and immersed the shards. I checked them every two hours or so and gently brushed the edges to dislodge the dirt. I repeated this process, changing the solution six times over a period of forty-eight hours, until I was satisfied that all the edges seemed free of stains. After washing them again in warm water I laid them out on a tray covered with tissue paper for forty-eight hours to dry.

It is often at this point, when edges are completely dry, that you can see if any really stubborn stains remain. A few stains were still evident and I treated these, after soaking again in cold water, with a solution of 20 vol hydrogen peroxide activated with a few drops of ammonia. I placed cotton wool strips soaked in this over the stains and wrapped them in airtight polythene bags to accelerate the process. I left them for two hours. I repeated this treatment twice before the stains had completely disappeared. I then rinsed the shards and allowed them to dry.

It is not advisable to use epoxy adhesives on porous earthenware; being less viscous they are more easily absorbed into the body of the object, which reduces their adhesive qualities and their reversibility. Instead I used a cellulose nitrate adhesive which can, if necessary, be thinned or dissolved with acetone. I applied very small amounts of the adhesive along the breaks, taping them together as I went, taking care not to 'trap' pieces out. Because the inside edges were so damaged it was hard to check for alignment in all the breaks, so I had to gauge most if this by the outside edges of each tile or by eye. They were then left to cure, standing vertically on an unbroken edge in a sand tray for twenty-four hours.

I then peeled the tape away and removed any excess adhesive with a scalpel or acetone. I used Polyfilla strengthened with poly vinyl acetate emulsion as a filler for the missing areas, as this most closely resembles an earthenware body. I dampened the edges of the missing areas to encourage adhesion before applying the paste. This has usually set hard enough in two hours to begin rubbing down with rifflers and flour paper – taking care not to scratch the surrounding glaze – until a smooth, even filling is achieved. I refilled the air holes etc. with fine-surface Polyfilla.

The tiles were now ready to be touched-in. I used a cold-setting urea formaldehyde/melamine based resin for this, which is a two-part clear varnish, which I coloured with artists' dry pigment to match the tiles' original glazes. Its consistency can be altered using thinners and the degree of shine adjusted with fumed silica, which acts as a matting agent. My studio has a very good north-facing light, which is essential for perfect colour matching; artificial light is too yellow or blue. Using an airbrush I sprayed a narrow, thinned coating of white resin along the joined and filled areas to even out the colour and show up any imperfections. This hardens in twenty-four hours. Then, with pigments and a matting agent, I matched the resin to the background glaze and sprayed this over the white, very lightly smoothing off in-between each coat, with very fine silicone carbide paper. This I adjusted with a glaze tint and in places applied specks of colour reproducing glaze spots, which would have happened naturally in the original firing. Then I touched-in the glaze colours of the design by hand, using fine brushes and a small sponge where appropriate, giving depth to the colour by using two or three coats where necessary.

To ensure the resin had hardened completely I left the tiles, covered with a plastic tray to keep off dust particles, for forty-eight hours. I then polished the painted areas with abrasive paste and finally waxed the tiles with microcrystalline wax for protection. The backs of the tiles were left with filling showing and not touched-in so that the restoration is not completely concealed for future reference. On the advice of Joe Dawes, the very dry, worn and cigarette burnt wooden frame was carefully cleaned with white spirit and given a coat of clear shellac varnish to seal it before the tiles were put back in place.

The second piece I treated was a large, decorated Provençal earthenware vessel with spout and handle from the studio. This was broken into twenty-eight pieces and had been previously restored using various different adhesives. Most of the vessel had come apart again and the glaze inside was flaking badly, probably because at one time it had been put on a pedestal in the middle of the small rectangular pond in the garden, where it had suffered from water and frost damage. The main problem was to remove all the old adhesives, which had been absorbed along the breaks into the body of the pot, without further damaging the glaze. Normally I would have soaked the shards to soften the adhesives, but this was not possible as it could have caused further flaking. After initial cleaning using swabs of cotton wool dampened with white spirit, I began to soften the old adhesives by applying lengths of cotton wool soaked in acetone along the breaks. I then sealed them in polythene bags to allow the fumes to penetrate. Acetone evaporates very rapidly even under these conditions so I periodically renewed the solvent by dripping more along the cotton wool. In most places I was able carefully to pull away the old adhesive; the rest I removed with a scalpel. I cleaned the edges with peroxide and ammonia. To consolidate the area on the inside of the pot, where the glaze was unstable and had flaked away, I used a solution of poly vinyl acetate granules dissolved in industrial methylated spirit 4:1, which I painted around under the edges of the flaking area and allowed to dry.

The shards were then ready to be assembled using cellulose nitrate adhesive. Because of the size and weight of the pot, I did this in two stages, to make the filling easier – first assembling the bottom half and then the top. A third of the spout was missing and two fairly large areas of the body. To replace these I took moulds from other parts of the pot using warmed dental wax strips pressed against areas of similar shape. After a few minutes, when the wax had cooled, I carefully removed it, dusted the inside of the moulds with talcum powder – to stop the filler sticking to them – and placed them over the missing areas, holding them down with tape. I then filled these with a mixture of Polyfilla and poly vinyl acetate emulsion, pressing it carefully into all the corners first and then filling up against the wax. After twenty-four hours I removed the wax and continued filling along the breaks. When this treatment was complete and rubbed down I assembled the two halves of the pot, still leaving the spout. It was then ready for me to test spray and paint using the same procedure as on the tiles. I continued until the background colour was complete, then bonded the spout to the body, filled and sprayed that join and continued hand painting-in the design. Then I finished off as before, polishing the painted areas with abrasive paste and waxing with microcrystalline wax for protection.

The third piece was a Wedgwood copy of an Omega Workshop earthenware charger decorated in a flecked blue glaze with white design, dated 1936. One large piece of the rim was broken and there was a running crack that had sprung apart from the inside corner of the break. It had not previously been restored. During biscuit firing a certain amount of tension is set up in the body of an object. If a break occurs this tension is occasionally released causing the crack or break to be sprung out of line, so as to appear not to fit when it is reassembled. The main problem when dealing with this is that the strength needed to push the springing back together again, and keep it in line, is too great for the normal method of taping to be affective. To get over this, I used a strong two-part epoxy adhesive and G-clamps to ease the edges back into line. I proceeded with the rest of the treatment as before until the painting stage when, as there were no large areas of filling to be disguised, I decided to hand paint rather than spray-out the joins.

These three pieces were back in place for the opening. Many more were to be treated in a similar manner later.

Chapter 10

Plans and Pictures

In January 1985 Michael Bagenal, the son of Barbara Bagenal who had looked after Clive Bell is his last years, sent two pictures his mother had left in her will to Charleston. They were Duncan Grant's portraits of Lytton Strachey and Saxon Sydney-Turner, which were very gratefully received by Debo. In February Quentin laid down, in a letter to her, what he felt their policy in relation to gifts and/or acquisitions should be. The priorities he set out were:

a. The retrieval or replacement of things which have been at Charleston and which we need if we are properly to restore the house; as for instance pictures which have been taken from Charleston as the result of bequests; furniture such as the big looking glass and the day bed from the studio.

b. Good examples of work by painters particularly associated with Charleston. Bell and Grant are obvious examples but arguably we might wish to acquire say a good specimen of the work of Edward Wolfe or a better example of Keith Baynes. But we do not need more pictures than we can show; a collection of Duncan's drawings or fifty paintings by Keith Baynes would be more than we can properly handle.

c. We do not need and should not acquire objects requiring special apparatus for conservation or special personnel. We are not a library or an archive, therefore, although we need books because Charleston was full of books, a hundred French paperbacks or twenty odd volumes of *The Strand Magazine*, which were indeed the kind of things that one found in the Charleston bookcases, would be preferable to a first edition of *The Waves*. In the same way documents: letters, manuscripts, etc. – things which ought to be accessible in places such as the University of Sussex or Kings College, Cambridge – should not be kept at Charleston; if they were, our keeping them would prove an embarrassment to both scholars and ourselves.

Following on from this letter, in June 1986, the Charleston Trust sought to acquire the Vanessa Bell *Self Portrait* she had painted in 1958. This was the first time the Trust had considered a major acquisition to return a work of art to the house. Debo consulted Anthony D'Offay to see how much money he thought needed to be raised. It seemed a daunting sum at the time but the picture would command a premium by

Self Portrait *by Vanessa Bell, bought by the Trust in 1986*

being part of Kenneth Clark's estate. Debo devoted considerable energy to raising the money. She asked Anthony D'Offay to bid on behalf of the Trust. Sitting beside him in the auction room her heart was in her mouth as the bidding rose steadily. Anthony secured what seemed to be the last bid and they waited an agonizingly long moment for the hammer to fall. Had there been another bid the picture would have been lost to Charleston. It was bought for £29,000 with help from the Art Fund, the Victoria and Albert Purchase Grant Fund and a generous donation from Margaret McDermott.

By May 1985 Quentin Bell was able to say in his Chairman's Report:

I am delighted to tell you, since my Chairman's Report a year ago, that a dramatic change has taken place at Charleston. The rooms are no longer stacked with packing cases and the walls bare with new plaster. During the spring a concerted effort took place. The whole house has been redecorated, builders' rubble removed, floors washed, panels, doors and fireplaces fitted back into place again. We have begun to reassemble the rooms, unpack fabrics, hang curtains and put out the furniture, objects and pictures. This will require painstaking and exacting work; it has been the restorers' task to emulate the effects of patina and age in the areas where new decoration has been necessary and a careful study of photographic material will ensure colours are matched and the rooms are reinstated as closely as possible.

Obviously some of the most important things to be conserved and returned to the house were the pictures. The ones in oil on canvas had been stored in the Towner Gallery in Eastbourne. There were about 120 of them. They had first been inspected by Sara Lee and Angelica Garnett in the middle of 1983. Sara describes this visit:

I looked briefly at each picture to get an idea of their condition. Very few were varnished. Some were unframed, and the ones which were were clumsily held in their frames by nails. Some showed signs of incipient flaking but none were in a dangerous state, so I felt they could remain where they were until a proper store could be built for them at Charleston. I noted that a few had been restored and had a rather shiny varnish on them.

This preliminary examination of the pictures took two hours. Angelica left me with the impression that she was concerned that the paintings (and their frames) should not return to Charleston looking shiny and too obviously recently restored. The frames had always been somewhat chipped and ill-fitting and were to remain so. In view of this, where bits of paint had flaked off, it would have been inappropriate to retouch the losses completely.

Work finally started in October 1984. The first task was to design and have built a storage space at Charleston. It was decided the attic room, adjoining Vanessa Bell's studio, would be used for this purpose as it was dry and would not have anyone walking through it. I asked the carpenter to construct several bays in which four or five paintings of similar size could be stacked, separated by double sheets of corrugated cardboard. On shelves above the bays small paintings could similarly be stacked.

The basis for treatment was as follows:

1. Examine the condition and make notes.
2. Remove the painting from its frame.
3. Consolidate flaking paint if necessary.
4. Clean dirt and grime off the surface.
5. Tone down or retouch losses.
6. If appropriate give the painting a sprayed-on coat of matt varnish.
7. Clean and secure the frame, removing old wall fittings and toning down losses.
8. Reframe the painting using mirror plates to hold it in its frame.

I knew that if there were no serious problems roughly thirty paintings could be treated in this way in a weekend with three restorers working on them. I knew that ten would have to be taken to London for treatment. We used the studio on the ground floor to

Sara Lee, responsible for the conservation of the paintings

work in and were kept very happy by a regular supply of coffee, delicious home-made cakes and wonderful lunches supplied by Vicki. We often worked ten hours a day. At the beginning of each weekend we would bring down about thirty paintings. Some of Duncan Grant's, where he had prepared the ground himself, were flaking badly. This was because the ground had insufficient medium so it had soaked up the oil from the paint. As a result there was almost no adhesion between the ground and paint layer. The worst example of this was in his *A Farmyard Scene*, which had to be treated in London. Where the flaking was less extensive it was treated at Charleston, introducing either gelatine (one part gelatine to ten parts distilled water) or a wax/resin mixture (cosmolloid wax and Laropal K80 resin) between the paint film and the ground or, in some cases, between the ground and the support.

Some paintings had tiny holes or tears which were not large enough to warrant lining. These were patched with nylon gossamer and Beva film. The nylon gossamer is very fine so the patch does not impress its shape onto the painting over the years, as canvas patches tend to do. The loss was then filled in with putty made from chalk, gelatine and a small amount of strand oil. The surface of the putty was given a texture to match that of the surrounding paint. This was then sealed with shellac and retouched. The extent of retouching varied from picture to picture. Many had fly droppings on them which had eaten into the paint – the droppings are acidic – leaving a small loss of paint when they were removed. Where these were in prominent places, such as the middle of someone's nose, they were retouched to match the surrounding paint. If they were in less obvious places they were toned down so they were not noticeable. Some paintings, such as a self-portrait by Duncan Grant, required the retouching of larger losses. For those we used egg tempera body colour followed by glazes of dry pigment mixed with Laropal K80 resin (a polcyclohexanone resin which has the optical properties of naturally occur-ring resins, such as Dammar, but which remains colourless with ageing).

It was decided that the paintings should not look varnished as they had not, apart from one or two, been varnished by Duncan or Vanessa. However, it was felt that there should be a coating on the paintings to protect them from superficial scratching and dirt. For this we used Laropal K80 resin in white spirit mixed with a small proportion of cosmolloid wax. When dry a thin film of this mixture has no gloss at all. The paint-ings that had previously been restored were too shiny, so the varnish, which was still soluble, was removed and replaced with the matt covering.

We had earlier removed four decorative paintings on unstretched canvas which were tacked to the panels of the wooden cupboard in the kitchen. Reinstating these was par-ticularly difficult. The kitchen is a working kitchen. The cupboard is next to the sink. The paintings would therefore be vulnerable to large changes in humidity as well as splashing from the sink. They were particularly vulnerable as they were painted on a very fine cotton ground with insufficient medium. The paintings were marouflaged using Beva adhesive onto acid-free card and held in the panel of the cupboard, which had been lined with acid-free paper, by double-sided tape attached to the back of the card. Reluctantly, as we would have liked to leave them as they were when Duncan Grant painted them, we put perspex sheets in front of the panels, separated from them by wooden batons.

The pictures on paper posed a multitude of different problems and were treated by Phillip Stevens and Heather Wood.

As one would expect there was enormous variety in these works, including early charcoal sketches, nineteenth- and twentieth-century prints, Victorian watercolours, collages, pastels, reproductions and even pencil drawings on picnic plates. Their problems ranged from the simple removal of acidic backings and surface dirt to quite major conservation, as in the case of the oil paintings on paper by Duncan Grant, which had been stuck onto hardboard.

An important part was played by the picture framers who remounted the pictures after conservation. The new acid-free mounts would have looked too uniform and out of place so a considerable effort was made to dirty them up! Facsimile acidic-looking bevels were painted on the window mounts, old inscriptions were reproduced and grubby finger marks were left on fly-spotted glass. Where new frames were needed these were made from old mouldings or painted to look contemporary.

By July 1985 things had progressed far enough for a notice to be drafted by Debo advertising the opening on 8 June the following year. At the same time she was planning another extravagant fundraising event: a trip for Americans, which would include a stay in London, visits to Kent and Sussex and finally going on the Orient Express to Venice. Her energy and dedication were unflagging. She wrote countless long and detailed letters, involving many in her enthusiasm for all aspects of the project. She also kept a close eye on the work in the house and paid meticulous attention to the accounts, which were kept by Piers St Aubyn. She authorized all payments and checked the amounts sent to the Trust by the Royal Oak Foundation. By the end of 1985 the total amount raised was £584,345.

Chapter 11

The Garden

'"How extraordinary that there should be such an unchanged spot in the world still,"
wrote Janie Bussy in 1947. Charleston had then been in Bloomsbury hands for over
thirty years.' This is how Peter Shepheard began the account of his work on the
garden. He went on: 'Even in 1984, half overgrown with grass and weeds, it was still
a hauntingly beautiful place, crying out for restoration.'

The garden in 1981, before restoration

Thanks to the interest and generosity of Mrs Lila Acheson Wallace and her representative William Barnabas McHenry, plans for the restoration of the garden had been securely laid. He said of her, after her death: 'She was interested in beautification. It's a tacky word, but she was fascinated with making things look better, restoring things that were once beautiful and bringing them back. She was not at all interested in social issues.' Their suggestion of using the landscape architect Peter Shepheard had been wholeheartedly endorsed by the Committee. At the same time a garden and grounds committee was formed, led by Penny Bardel. The other members were: Hugh Lee, who had kept the grass cut and the worst of the 'volunteers' in check; Vicki Walton, who had worked in the garden ever since she had lived at Charleston; Angelica Garnett, who had known the garden all her life and had planted a number of perennials when she lived there from 1978 to1980; and Olivier Bell, who had come with her children to stay at Charleston during the 1950s.

Peter Shepheard takes up the story:

Restoration is fraught with difficulty. It is easy, especially with gardens, to supplant what once existed by a new thing – sometimes a good thing, but always tending to stand in the way of the old thing. But here at Charleston there was ample witness to its former state. Charleston was created by artists and writers who left a vivid picture not only of the place but of the life it sheltered. Their visitors too wrote and painted, and everyone seemed to take photographs. There are still those of the present generation who spent their childhood in the garden – Angelica Garnett and Quentin Bell – and those who came later and knew it in its final maturity, like Olivier Bell and Richard Shone. And then there are the photographs, especially Vanessa's 'family album' of the inhabitants of the garden and their children and visitors. By peeking between the people one can see most of the detail of the garden – flowers, paths, edgings, ponds and sculptures.

From all this and from the paintings and writings, a vivid picture emerged of the character of the place. One could see the 'great variegated quilt of asters and artichokes' and the red admiral butterflies, for which we were careful to preserve the nettles in the cattle-yard drain. One could see Vanessa with her passion for colour having the garden one year 'in a scheme of reds – zinnias, dahlias, scabious, salpiglossis and red hollyhocks'. It was a painter's garden, full of paintable flowers. It was a garden for people to sit and talk and paint in. But the flowers took up most of the space. People sat on the terrace, on the small lawn or in the piazza. The lawn – only one eighth of the area between the walls – was bordered by a low hedge of cotton lavender – as if to protect the flowers from the people.

The design of the garden was simple, even a little stiff, between its flint walls; a pattern of straight paths and rectangular beds studded with ancient apple trees , all slightly overlaid with a teeming mass of flowers. It was an apotheosis of the traditional English cottage garden. Angelica Garnett, Anne Olivier Bell and Richard Shone all made lists of the plants they remembered at different periods of the garden's history – not the new 'improved' hybrids, but the old permanent flowers of the cottage garden: peonies, poppies, Michaelmas daisies and columbines; here and there classical plants of the Mediterranean: asphodel, acanthus, fig, vine; traditional edging plants: cotton lavender, and Mrs Sinkins pinks; many silver and grey plants: lamb's ears, phlomis and the great silvery willows by the pond. And, of course, the walls were laden with plants: roses, clematis and pears and, on the house corner, Duncan Grant's favourite *hydrangea petiolaris*. It was a garden filled to overflowing, the plants jostling and blending with one another as in a meadow, not too precise but in a sweet disorder.

The first step was to restore the boundary walls. Photographs were taken of their whole length inside and out. Ivy was removed and the roses and other climbers eased off the walls and laid down ready for refixing. All loose masonry – most of the facings and all of the brick courses crowning the wall – was cut off and what remained was cleaned with a strong jet of water, leaving a core of stones and flint on a good foundation. The whole was then refaced using old and new flints and bricks, keeping as close as possible to the original pattern.

This work was undertaken by the builders H.F. Wilson Ltd. Penny Bardel continues the story:

Quentin and Olivier Bell against the rebuilt wall

In rebuilding the perimeter wall we had omitted three non-functional buttresses on the interior of the west wall, which had certainly been hasty patch-ups amateurishly added long after the building of the original wall. As soon as the new wall, without its buttresses, was complete everyone felt that it had been unacceptably changed. They missed the familiar rhythmic sequence of the buttresses along that portion of the wall. So, at some additional cost, they were reinstated and the consensus since has been that they do indeed 'belong' in the garden.

The next phase was to reinstate the paths and beds; but before this was tackled a drainage system from the house was taken across the garden. Corinne Bennett explains:

The drainage system for both surface and foul water were found to be faulty and leaking and had to be almost entirely renewed. The method of disposal of the sewage was, as one might expect, rather ill defined and in fact the exact position of the existing cesspool could not be found. A completely new septic tank and disposal area were therefore provided to the north-west of the house beyond the car park which was formed there. The exact route of the new drainage ran through the garden and was worked out in conjunction with Sir Peter Shepheard. A lead drain was also laid around the south, east and west sides of the house to try to prevent water from the farm running below the foundations.

Peter Shepheard continues:

The paths and beds had to be freed from the grass which had completely covered most of them, especially on the west side. No accurate plan of the garden existed; the original layout was gradually revealed by carefully removing the grass to find traces of the gravel paths and their brick edgings. Most of the bricks had disappeared through damage by frost. The new edgings, in frost-proof bricks which matched the colour of the old, were laid on narrow concrete foundations. The paths are of crushed stone to match as closely as possible the original pebbles from the Channel beaches.

The restoration of the mosaic pavement of the piazza in the north-east corner of the garden was tricky. Tough weeds, dandelions and dock and goutweed (ground elder), had invaded the pattern and we had to use weed killer. The mosaic panels – broken crockery pressed into cement mortar – were surprisingly sound; but the thin concrete panels and the brick dividing lines had been broken up by frost. They were rebuilt in concrete 4 inches thick, with lines of frost-proof bricks. We were careful to keep the exact shapes of the original layout with its rough texture and irregular slopes.

In the same cautious way we rebuilt the arbour outside Duncan Grant's studio in the south-west corner, following the original primitive but effective design in peeled fir poles, with steel tubes overhead to carry the ancient grapevine. To the west of the studio is the little separate court built in 1925 and called Duncan's Folly, a charming outdoor room to which the party used to gravitate on summer evenings to get the benefit of the westerly sun. This too we restored, renewing its pergola and its floor of crushed stone, shaping its rampant figs and replanting its narrow flower beds with humble but delicious plants: periwinkle, bluebells, *corydalis lutea* and the little black iris *hermodactylis tuberosa*.

The great flower beds of the walled garden, now framed by their new paths, still contained some of their original plants, heavily overgrown by grass and weeds. We left some of these *in situ*, especially old-established clumps of peony, red-hot poker and oriental poppy. Others, rescued from the weeds, were kept for replanting. The weeds were then cleared, not with chemicals but by hand-digging the whole area three or four times. The replanting plan contained over a hundred species of plants of which about thirty were the existing originals. The new plants were drawn from the recollection of the people who knew the garden in its prime, plus other plants which I thought likely to have been known to Vanessa Bell. Some of these fine old Edwardian plants were surprisingly difficult to find and had to be hunted down in specialist nurseries.

Outside the walled garden on the east side lie the orchard and the pond, where less work was needed. We remade the path and the flower bed outside the east wall and renewed the terrace by the front door. We removed a few intrusive plum trees from the orchard; added a walnut tree to replace one, now lost, which Duncan Grant had planted in the paddock, north of the garden; and planted bulbs in the grass. We did some pruning and tidying of the poplars and willows to the north of the pond and removed an aggressive sycamore maple which was threatening the big yew tree on the north bank. We thinned the saplings on the east side of the pond and removed some shrubs from the south-west bank to improve the view of the fields to the east. The pond itself had suffered from the drying up of its tiny feeding pipe. We raised the water level by repairing the dam at the outlet but we hope to find a new source of water to keep the pond full in the summer.

Originally the walled garden was sheltered on the west and north by huge elms. All except two had died long ago from the Dutch disease and these two died as we began work on the garden. We have replaced them with eighteen grey poplars – *populus cinerea* – which arrange themselves conveniently round the car park, which hides behind the west wall. They will provide a high screen of silvery foliage to protect the garden from the west wind which strikes along the north flank of Firle Beacon. A hawthorn hedge was planted along the whole boundary, including the car park and the orchard. This will eventually be laid in the traditional manner to make a low, stock-proof fence over which can be seen the beautiful countryside to the north.

A charming feature of the garden was the collection of playful sculptures: one by Duncan Grant of a male torso; some by Quentin Bell and a whole group of others, mostly in plaster, which Duncan had got from the local art school. Ten of these were classical heads which stood on top of the walls looking outwards; all but three of these had melted in the rain and frost. They were recast and Quentin made a fourth. He also found the pretty nude – a copy of one by Giovanni de Bologna – which terminates the western path, and the torso of Venus in the orchard. The other sculptures in the orchard had been made by Quentin. Three had been there for some time: the Spink in carved red brickwork, Pomona with her bucket of apples on her head and a female figure in ciment fondu standing by the pond. The levitating lady by the pond was added in 1983. He also remade the urns which crown the piers of the front gate. There is a pleasing head of Vanessa's mother, Julia Stephen, by the sculptor Baron Marochetti, on the terrace outside Duncan Grant's studio.

All the restoration in the garden except the rebuilding of the walls was undertaken by Clifton Nurseries in London. There were two teams: one responsible for hard landscaping – paths and edging – the other soft landscaping – the beds and plants. The latter was led by Mark Divall. He was involved in the clearing and original cultivation of the garden, but the autumn planting in 1985 had to be done by the other team, as he had been called back to London. It was in the following year, on 1 April, that Mark took up the job of Charleston's keeper of gardens and grounds. He later wrote:

The garden in April 1986

I remember wondering at the time if there was any significance in that date. I hadn't seen the garden since late the previous summer and was now struck by how desolate it looked. We were in the middle of a dismal spring which had followed a severe winter. The pond was frozen solid for several weeks, which meant that Charleston's resident ducks had to be kept in the walled garden to protect them from foxes. The result was that the previously turned soil was now padded down and any green shoots brave and strong enough to push their way up to the surface were nibbled off.

When the pond thawed and the ducks were persuaded to leave the walled garden, a start had to be made to prepare for the opening, now only two months away. Any thoughts of the wisdom of leaving my safer London job were pushed to the back of my mind by the urgency of work and the shortness of time in which to do it. Imperceptibly at first, the plants began to grow, and as their growth increased so did my optimism that we would have some semblance of the garden, so many people had worked towards creating, in time for the opening of the house in June.

The first task was to turn over the surface of the soil to help warm up the topsoil and, at the same time, mark out the areas that still needed planting. It was apparent straight away that several groups of plants had not survived the winter very well, notably the Japanese anemone, anchusa and crinums. As a result of these casualties and the unavailability of replacements, some regrouping of plants was necessary and the resulting empty areas were filled with plants such as lavatera, potentilla, night-scented stocks and tobacco plants.

Several groups of plants had deliberately been left for planting until early spring, either because of their questionable hardiness or because they had been unobtainable in the autumn. One of these was the old fashioned pink, Mrs Sinkins, of which nearly five hundred were planted. It turned out later that over a hundred of these were not Mrs Sinkins at all but Haytors White, which illustrated the difficulty there sometimes is in obtaining large numbers of identical plants.

One of the less charming aspects of gardening is that, as soon as things start to grow in the spring, weeds always seem to be slightly ahead of the more desirable plants. Even though, during the initial cultivation, great efforts had been made to get rid of the perennial weeds, such as ground elder, couch grass and bindweed, in late April and early May, almost three weeks were spent weeding the walled garden with a hand fork to remove, as far as possible, every last trace of these unwelcome residents. Some large clumps of original plants, such as red hot poker and shasta daisy had not been disturbed earlier, for fear of damaging them, and were still riddled with ground elder. Although by early May it was getting late, these were lifted and all the soil removed from their roots so that every last piece of ground elder could be eliminated. The cool, wet spring was helpful in re-establishing these plants. This very methodical first weeding was certainly worthwhile, as later weed growth was easily kept in check.

During these first months I was pleasantly surprised by how small a problem pest and disease control was compared with my previous gardening experience in London. I am convinced a major factor in this is allowing the natural predators of pests, such as aphids, to do the work of pesticides. During the whole of the first summer the only one used was the natural pesticide pyrethrum. Large quantities of farmyard manure were added to the soil during the initial cultivation and all the fertilizers used were organic, which created good soil structure with a thriving community of organisms. This 'live

Angelica Seated at the Charleston Studio Door *by Vanessa Bell, showing the garden at its most abundant*

and let live' philosophy was severely tested when a rabbit took up residence in the walled garden and started eating all the new young shoots of the plants it liked. Fortunately, after a few half-hearted attempts, it was successfully evicted.

One of the largest apple trees had looked quite sick the previous summer and did not make it through the winter. It was decided not to remove it for this first summer as it would so change the overall skyline. However, as the branches became brittle and broke off, it had to be reduced to a stump. Nasturtiums were successfully encouraged to grow up and over it. The stump was later removed and a new apple tree planted to take its place.

By late June, as growth increased and the garden began to take on a surprisingly mature look, any early doubts I had had about working at Charleston had faded away. My major fear before taking on the job was that I would have very little latitude for expressing by own interpretation of how the garden should develop. But essentially the continuing restoration of the garden will depend on a sympathetic but not all-consuming feel for how it originally evolved, which would have been a gradual emergence of form and colour rather than an elaborately prearranged and meticulous plan. As all gardeners know, the many vagaries of climate, soil and other elements play their own part in what eventually emerges. One of the many rewarding aspects of working at Charleston has been the interest taken in the garden's re-emergence by those who lived and grew up here and those who used to visit. I am sure this interest will ensure the reality of the garden will never be too far away from its creative heyday.

The garden in summer 1986

The restoration of the garden was made possible by the generosity of Mrs Lila Acheson Wallace. She was sadly too infirm to visit Charleston herself; but, as the planning and actual work on the garden proceeded, Mr William Barnabas McHenry, on her behalf and after her death, came repeatedly to see the progress at first hand. He spent time with Debo, Quentin, Olivier, Sir Peter and all the others involved in the project. Their enthusiasm and delight and the sheer beauty and success of the restoration of the garden encouraged him to fund the whole project. This generosity is acknowledged by a plaque, made by Quentin, fixed near the gate on the south wall of the garden.

Plaque acknowledging the generosity of Lila Acheson Wallace,
who made the restoration of the garden possible

Chapter 12

Towards the Opening

In November 1985 the Savoy Group of hotels – which had been founded on the music of Gilbert and Sullivan – sponsored an exhibition in Washington DC entitled *The Treasure Houses of Great Britain*. It had originally been planned to reconstruct one of the Charleston rooms for it, but this proved technically too difficult. However, Debo had kept in touch with them and, on 1 January 1986, they promised $10,000 as major sponsors of a second symposium to take place in Dallas in March. They put out a beautifully designed press release, which was not only about Dallas, but also gave details of the Treasure Hunt they were organizing, in conjunction with British Caledonian Airways and the National Trust, for Americans to visit the Treasure Houses of Great Britain in late October. This did not, in the end, materialize.

When Debo had first mooted a second visit to Dallas it was not greeted with enthusiasm by some of the Committee. If she had followed their advice and that of *The Times* she would certainly not have gone ahead with it. A comment in the newspaper, on 1 February, under the heading 'Culture Club' and accompanied by photographs of Quentin Bell and Hugh Casson, said:

> Oh for the optimism of Quentin Bell and Sir Hugh Casson! Shortly this genial pair of ancients fly out to Dallas in search of cultured folk and £250,000 to help preserve Charleston the fabled country home of the Bloomsbury group in Sussex. Casson stoutly defends the notion of culture in Dallas. 'Did you know they had a Left Bank there?' he asks. I went looking for it but couldn't find it.

A review of the event by Patsy Swank, a connoisseur of culture in the United States, bears witness to its success:

> The singular air of Bloomsbury came back to Texas last week in an extraordinary five days at the Dallas Museum of Art and the Fort Worth Museum, during which the aura of Virginia and Leonard Woolf, Vanessa and Clive Bell, Duncan Grant and the whole train of notable figures who surrounded them was re-created by their kin, their contemporaries and their admirers. . . .
> As is so often the case, the influence of the Bloomsbury group on so many levels of

British life and culture was not fully recognized until most of them were dead. Recollection, conversation, and the exchange of ideas – dominant elements of their own lives – were brought to Dallas by Vanessa Bell's daughter Angelica Bell Garnett, and her son Quentin Bell, in two irreplaceable discussions of their lives as children in both London and Charleston. The contemporary novelist Margaret Drabble spoke of Virginia Woolf's work, Richard Shone, Associate Editor of the *Burlington Magazine*, talked of the importance and productivity of Vanessa and Clive Bell, of Duncan Grant, Roger Fry, and other artists whose lives touched or were touched by Charleston Farmhouse. The day was opened and closed by the witty remarks of Sir Hugh Casson, a former president of the Royal Academy of Arts.

The restoration itself was reported by Deborah Gage, a specialist in eighteenth century art, who is also the vital and dynamic co-ordinator of The Charleston Trust (and on whose family land Charleston is located). Sir Peter Shepheard, London planner and landscape architect (and dean emeritus of the Graduate School of Fine Arts at the University of Pennsylvania), told of the joys and difficulties in re-creating the garden which was a pivotal part of life at Charleston.

The Dallas weekend closed with a reading of *Freshwater*, a hilarious spoof that Virginia Woolf had written in 1923 and revised in January 1935 for a series of theatrical evenings to celebrate the sixteenth birthday of her niece Angelica, who took part. Woolf in her diary called it 'an unbuttoned, laughing evening'. The more recent 'unbuttoned' evening in Dallas was the kind that might never happen again.

The play concern's Woolf's aunt, the early woman photographer Julia Margaret Cameron (played by Angelica Bell Garnett), and her household, which bears a suspicious similarity to the one at Charleston. Members of the household included: the young actress Ellen Terry, played by Lynn Redgrave; Julia's husband, Charles, played by Michael Holroyd; the housemaid, who was constantly busy in the kitchen with the Earl of Dudley, was played by Margaret Drabble; Lord Alfred Tennyson was Quentin Bell; the painter George Frederick Watts was Hugh Casson; and Queen Victoria, Anne Olivier Bell. Marshalling them all was the brilliant actor Robert Hardy, best known here as the veterinarian in the TV series *All Creatures Great and Small*. One does not usually think of Virginia Woolf as being side-splitting. Those who were in attendance on Sunday evening now can.

The whole event was underwritten by a number of sponsors in addition to the Savoy Group. The House of Harry Winston made available, on sale or return, silver objects to be auctioned at a gala dinner. Other supporters included British Caledonian Airways, who gave free transport to the participants, and Ellen Terry Realtors, who paid for the production of *Freshwater*. It was one of the outstanding examples of Debo's ability to raise international awareness of Charleston at the same time as financial support for its restoration.

By January it had become clear the damp problem in the house had not been solved. There was rising damp in the dining room and the garden room. This meant that £5,000 had to be put aside to pay for a damp proof course in these two rooms; it also meant there was no question of replacing the decorated wall surfaces in these rooms. It was decided that the opening should be in two stages: the first in June of that year and the second in April the following year, by which time it was hoped all the rooms would be completed. In the event this proved to be over-optimistic.

Geraldine Guest, who had been working throughout the winter on various things, takes up the story:

Pauline Plummer, who oversaw the interior restoration, in the studio

In the early spring of 1986 I had the pleasure of meeting and working with Joe Dawes, the wood restorer. He had returned to refit various decorated panels he had been treating in his studio. There was still a lot of unpainted furniture to be worked on, so, after touching-in and distressing areas left obvious when Joe had finished refitting the panels, I helped with cleaning, French polishing and waxing furniture. I also distressed and colour-matched stretchers, for holding the cane seats that Joe had renewed in places, on the six red lacquer Omega chairs from the dining room. When Pauline and her team returned at Easter, I continued removing protective wax paper from the studio mantelshelf before consolidating and touching it in.

Pauline Plummer continues:

At one time there were ten people at work in the house alone: conservators, craftsmen, volunteers, not to mention the visiting Telecom engineer. I found that my role was reduced to running continually from the furthest point of the ground floor to the corresponding area upstairs as each in turn of the ten workers wanted advice on some problem. It was totally exhausting and I became quite punch-drunk, but how glad I was that everyone did ask, rather than risk making incorrect decisions. The atmosphere of enthusiasm and positive determination to achieve the best possible result was so invigorating it helped to carry us through. The other factor was Vicki's great kindness and helpfulness in looking after us and ministering to our needs with never failing cheerfulness.

I had fought long and hard for authentic light switches and power points. The changing shapes of light switches has become a close study for all concerned at Charleston. Thanks to a number of interested electricians and friends who had had their houses rewired we now have a large collection of fittings of the correct period, with enough spare to furnish a museum. Power points were another matter. The present regulations insist on their being placed well above the skirting boards. The originals are now blanks, screwed in the old positions, while the live sockets are masked by panels painted to match the walls.

In the last few weeks before the house opened, when the major works were complete, we were more and more aware of the little things which were anachronistic. My cares ranged from the replacement of plastic lavatory cisterns with heavy cast iron ones to finding the right design of window catches and door latches; ensuring that lamp holders were brown Bakelite hung on fabric-covered cables and that light pulls in the bathroom and lavatories were as old as possible.

The paper lantern over the bulb outside the spare room, which had once shown the faces of the sun and moon in garish blue and yellow, was torn beyond repair, but with triumph I discovered they were still available in toy shops. The new one had to be distressed – it was supposed to be thirty years old!

Wilma Harper elaborates on the 'distressing' techniques:

Having worked on the overall restoration programme I knew the situation of each item and was sympathetic to the degree of distressing necessary in order to make the redecorated rooms and newly restored furniture and fittings blend harmoniously together. Anyone entering a room after it had been finished might not have been aware that some 'ageing down' had taken place. Much of the uneven character of the walls had been lost with replastering and therefore, where there was any indication of a slight bump or incline these were emphasized. Other areas that received attention were above light bulbs, where the walls meet the ceiling and the corners around the edge of the windows.

To achieve superficial distressing a weak solution of size mixed with whiting, raw umber and ivory black was sprayed on to a given area using a Humbrol hand spray. (A weak solution of size meant that the distemper could be rubbed off again if necessary). The sprayed distemper was then worked into the underlying paint with fingertips, palms or a soft brush and, where necessary, the effect consolidated with a further spraying of a stronger solution of size on its own. The size was made of 15 gm of rabbit-skin glue or 8 gm of powdered gelatine in a pint of water. The occasional fly marks near and around the windows were added knowing full well that Charleston's own flies would in time follow on and take over where we left off.

The conservation of the painted wall surfaces had been controversial from the start, especially the ones in the dining room and the garden room. Debo thought it was vital it should go ahead because of the conditions of the Historic Buildings Council grant and, as important, to preserve the integrity of the original surfaces. Others were not sure it was worth it. This disagreement was to rumble on for some time to come. When they had been successfully removed from the walls they were stored at Bonhams in London; from there they were taken to Phillip Stevens's workshop for conservation. They had been moved to his studio in October 1985. The first job was to sort them. Some had been so damaged by damp, particularly those in the garden room and dining room, that there was no possibility of saving them. These were put aside and later archived at Charleston. Phillip Stevens describes the stages that would have to be gone through before the others were ready to be rehung:

Removing the layers of old wallpaper and plaster from the backs of each section was a very long and dusty job. Then, while face down, tears were repaired with narrow strips of Japanese paper and fragments reattached. Sheets of Japanese tissue, impregnated with thymol, were interleaved between the sections to treat any mould which was still present; these were then left in sealed bags for a week.

Consolidation of the flaking paint layer was a constant preoccupation from start to finish. Each paper had its own problems and different fixatives and consolidants were

Removing layers of old paper and plaster from murals in Phillip Stevens's workshop

experimented with. The heavy, thick flakes of the dining room paper were quite easy to refix using a dry sodium alginate and arrowroot paste or a 5% methyl cellulose. Laying this paper onto a new backing also helped consolidation as we could let the adhesive penetrate from the back without danger of staining.

The tiny crumbly flakes of more powdery areas were sprayed with a ¼% hot gelatine solution which penetrated the paint film and soaked through to reattach it to the paper. A 2% solution of Klucel G in isopropyl alcohol was useful as it reduced the risk of staining and was used where one paint layer was lifting from another, as in the heavily stencilled motifs of the garden room paper. Fixing individual flakes was incredibly time consuming.

Different acid-free Japanese papers were chosen for the backings to give appropriate strength and where necessary two layers were laminated together to give an even thickness. A 5% methyl cellulose solution was used for laying down, and drying out was done under pressure as quickly as possible. Missing areas were repaired with matching papers making an infill on the front which was then toned and facsimiled. Some of the areas where there was paint loss were also toned.

Returning the murals to the house was the most enjoyable part of the work. Work started in the spare room in March 1986. The walls were now lined with acid-free Archive Text. The column sections were put up first, again using a 5% methyl cellulose adhesive, and then the arches were fitted in between. There were some slight changes in the size of the walls due to the replastering and some small gaps had to be filled where the slope of the ceiling had changed. The light switches seemed to have been a

Clive Bell's bedroom in 1986 showing conserved panel and reproduced Grapes fabric

little restless and had crept up the wall a couple of centimetres, but apart from this the rehanging was successful. The lining paper borders were trimmed and the room was then ready for the infill colour to be painted.

The decorated paper panel from Clive Bell's bedroom had been removed from its door and repaired. It was then laid down on a new acid-free backing board and some of the border strips were facsimiled.

The debate in April was not about the dining room and the garden room papers but about the dog and the cockerel in the library. These had originally been painted for Vanessa by Duncan when this was her bedroom. The dog was to guard her, the cockerel to wake her up. By 1984 they were in a very sorry state. At first it was thought they would have to be treated *in situ*, but, as Phillip Stevens describes, this proved impossible:

Painted thinly onto very thin paper they had sustained much paint loss over the years and been patched and retouched many times. Cracking in the wall and the generally poor condition of the underlying plaster made it necessary to remove the two panels in order to provide them with a better support. They were so fragile they had to be repeatedly spray-fixed with a ¼% gelatine solution before, during and after removal. The paint film was so brittle that any slight flexing of the paper could cause flaking. Further consolidation was done in the studio where they were laid onto a Japanese tissue support. Missing areas were repaired and a facsimile done in areas of paint loss.

Part of the dog, painted by Duncan Grant, before conservation

Originally the painted wall surfaces had been given priority over these because they would have to be rehung; also they had all sustained damage from fungal growth while they had been in storage so it seemed sensible and economical to treat all the surfaces to prevent further damage. As two of the more important rooms downstairs would be unavoidably unfinished because of the damp problem, Quentin Bell felt it was essential that the upstairs rooms should be complete. He wanted the dog and the cockerel to be put in place even if they had to be removed again to finish their conservation. Debo responded to this suggestion in a long letter to him of which the following is a part:

The bird and the dog are now undergoing conservation at Phillip's studio – they are working flat out and scheduled to complete for the end of May. If they fall behind schedule for the press day or the opening they will go up fairly soon thereafter. We must not take risks or jeopardise safety for the sake of pleasing the public.

I would not be at all happy about your proposition to replace the bird and the dog as a temporary measure. As I have explained to everyone in previous meetings, we are dealing with extraordinarily fragile surfaces and therefore we must ensure that we get everything right, because we will not have a second chance. Not only would the bird and dog suffer as a result of going up and being taken down again, but this would also add to our expense. It should be borne in mind that they are the most *delicate* of all the surfaces.

We have prepared everyone for the fact the house will not be completely finished by phasing the opening in two stages, this is dealt with in our press release and I suggest the press is addressed to this effect.

You mentioned you feel the costs of restoration are unwarranted and we are treating everything like Leonardo cartoons. The reason why the Charleston Trust came into being was to preserve Charleston and its contents in perpetuity. Therefore there are certain disciplines that have to be undertaken to ensure the works are stable. The reason why the wallpapers are so expensive to deal with is their sheer scale and the work thereby involved. You and I had different points of view when I told you I regarded the wallpapers as the most important objects in the house. Apart form the ambience and setting, surely what will be of interest to future generations is *how much* we have been able to save of the original. After all we do state that it was at Charleston the decorative schemes by Bell and Grant found their finest and most characteristic flowering – and this will always be part of the fascination. If we had reproduced the decorative surfaces totally in facsimile, we might just as well have forsaken the idea of preserving

The dog after conservation

Charleston and reconstructed some rooms at, say, the V&A?

Everyone has worked very hard and we shall certainly have a good show for everyone to see when we open the front door at Charleston on June 7. Remember the surprise and how marvellous the house looked on the last Open Day and then we were not nearly so far forward as we are now. It truly does not matter that the house is not finished. That is why we are announcing the opening in two stages. I have often visited places where work is still in hand – it is fascinating watching it happen.

Phillip Stevens completes the story of the conservation of what had come to be called the bird and the dog:

Even after extensive attempts to stop the flaking it was decided that the paintings were far too frail to be left exposed and returned directly to the walls. If protected only on the front from abrasions any temperature, humidity or air flow changes could still cause future problems. We reluctantly decided that the only solution was to construct a more protective box frame that would be as unobtrusive as possible. Two rigid, glazed supports were lined with acid-free board; acid-free fillets were made to hold the pictures away from the glass. The thin metal frames were covered with Japanese paper and both this and the fillets were painted to tone in with the borders of each picture. This left light refraction on the glass the only visual disturbance but the long term safety of the pictures was assured.

In May a press release went out and gained a considerable amount of press coverage, which was even greater after the press day on 25 May. The last word goes to Pauline Plummer:

In the last weeks, when the conservators' work was virtually completed and it remained only to put the finishing touches, Quentin and Olivier Bell came frequently and their critical and sympathetic comments were invaluable.

The work of washing, polishing, furnishing, hanging curtains, making fittings, replacing photos and postcards on the studio mantelpiece and tucked into the mirror, putting half full bottles and glasses on tables, throwing cigarette butts where they'd always been in the front of the pither stove, everything to make it looked lived in, continued frenziedly for several more weeks until the great day of the opening finally arrived.

It was not until a few weeks later that I had time to go alone round the house and stand silently to feel the impact of what we had achieved. Every corner, every surface had received our care. We had all worked and worried for so long to perfect it. It was done and the atmosphere of the house was almost tangible.

On the day it opened 480 people came to see the house.

Chapter 13

The Opening and After

In November 1985 Tina Jeffrey had been appointed as Administrator. When the house opened on 8 June the entrance and shop were in the garden room. Visitors walked in through the French windows. Tina stood behind a counter to their left and sold tickets for £1.50. A few postcards, posters and books were for sale and a bell was rung to announce the start of each tour. The 'guidebook' consisted of six double-sided, mimeographed pages stapled together. The entry for the garden room began: 'Continuing problems with rising damp, combined with a severe shortage of funds, has prevented the completing of this room. It is hoped the hand-painted wallpapers (seen in the photographs on display) will be reinstated, together with the painted over-mantel panel.' The lack of completion also, of course, applied to the painted wall surfaces in the dining room.

Many of the early visitors were knowledgeable about the people who had lived and worked in the house. There was a lot of swapping of information, pleasure and opinions as they walked round the rooms. It was as though old friends were meeting after a number of years, and finding they still had much in common. Those who had been in the house during one of the Open Days, when it was bare of most of its contents, were amazed at the transformation of it and of the garden. It was described as 'one of the most difficult and imaginative feats of restoration current in Britain'. The 480 people, who were there on the opening day, showed their admiration, which was reflected in a host of illustrated articles in newspapers and magazines both in Britain and in the United States. This publicity resulted in a steady stream of visitors. By the end of the year around 12,000 people had come to look at the house and garden.

The first, and almost certainly the most exciting, part of the restoration was complete; but Debo had always held onto two central aims, which were not be compromised: to conserve all the painted wall surfaces and to have a separate visitors' centre. Neither of these had been accomplished. The latter had, for obvious reasons, been left in the background until the majority of the work in the house was finished. She felt this domestic jewel should not be tarnished by having one of the central rooms used as an area to dispense tickets. Both of these projects required considerable additional funds.

She wrote about these points in a letter to Nigel Nicolson, who had been in

America at the time of the opening. After telling him of its success she continues:

On the financial side things are not so rosy. We have run over budget in all areas which has necessitated selling our securities and taking out a loan with Barclays Bank. (Although the three Trustees have given their personal guarantee, all the Committee members have a collective responsibility). Dallas failed to produce immediate income (though there are promises in hand) and therefore we have stopped work on the next stages. The wallpapers will prove far more costly than estimated and a further £35,000 will be needed to complete the garden room and the dining room. If this money is not found by August or early September, we will not be able to open next April for the 1987 season. Help has come in other respects: for example, Paul Mellon has just come forward with an offer of $50,000 to build a visitors' centre.

She elaborated on this last point in a letter to Piers St Aubyn on the same day:

I met with Strutt and Parker at the Charleston Barn last Monday to assess and discuss the position concerning the restoration of the barn and our proposed Visitors' Centre. [Part of the barn had been destroyed by fire just before the Trust bought the house in 1981 and the Firle Estate had promised to restore it.] They suggested offering us the cowshed which is the building that runs alongside our access road to the car park, which we could convert into a Visitors' Centre.... With the money the Firle Estate would obtain for the cowshed they would restore the Charleston Barn. I am now waiting for Strutt and Parker to come back with a formal offer and price for the cowshed and will then obtain an estimate for its conversion. Of course I have kept Paul Mellon fully briefed and he is now waiting for me to come back with figures. The reason I mention this is because until we have put in a final proposal to Paul Mellon his funds will not be forthcoming.

The other problem which had to be resolved at this time was the chairmanship of the Trust. Quentin Bell had made it clear in the spring that he wanted to resign in the summer. At the end of her letter to Nigel Nicolson she wrote:

Quentin has now stepped down as Chairman. After long deliberations we felt that we did not want to go outside the Committee for a new chairman. You wrote to say that you would be agreeable to taking on the Vice Chairmanship for another year and I am writing to ask whether you would in fact take on the Chairmanship? There could be no better person and we left the position open at the AGM hoping that you would accept!

In his reply he said: 'I do *not* think I can take on the Chairmanship. You need a brighter, younger person to handle the financial situation. I'm such a bad beggar!'

Olivier Bell had already made it clear that she did not want the position, which left them with a dilemma. Later in the year Noel Annan and Jeremy Hutchinson were approached but both turned it down saying, like Nigel Nicolson, they were too old. For the time being, the attempt to find a replacement was left, and Nigel Nicolson agreed to be acting as well as vice-chairman for a year. He, too, would then resign.

He wrote to Debo once again, querying the escalating cost of conserving the decorated wall surfaces. His views were backed up in a letter from Helen Lowenthal. Debo wrote back in no uncertain terms:

I realize as you have not had the day to day insight concerning the working and technical aspects relating to the decorated wall surfaces, it is difficult to fairly assess the position. I have no reason whatsoever to doubt the integrity of Phillip Stevens, or his charges. Where he has made an error he has not put in for time or materials. His charge out rate is £20 per hour inclusive of materials – my garage mechanic charges £27 per hour plus materials! There is no need to emphasize which is the more skilled task!

Where the problem has in fact arisen is in estimating the work. The first estimate (for £15,000) was given when the wall surfaces were up on the walls. Since they have been removed it has been discovered that they adhered to many layers of brittle and deteriorated wallpaper underneath, all of which had to be scraped off, layer by layer to the pigment surface. This had to be done and this is what cost the money. The entire job, i.e. five rooms, will eventually work out in the region of £80,000.

It was the declared object of the Trust to preserve Charleston and its contents. You might find Quentin and Olivier would put forward the argument that the walls should simply be re-stencilled. If this kind of attitude is adopted frankly I do not see any reason to save Charleston, you might just as well make up a pastiche in a museum somewhere. I feel I would be blamed by future generations for the wanton destruction of original works of art. What will be of interest to future generations is *how much* we have been able to save – and you will find Richard, Peter, Simon and myself regard the decorated wall surfaces as the most important element of all at Charleston.

On 9 July Nigel Nicolson agreed that there was no point in looking to stop the conservation at this point. However, the problem of the rising damp had still not been solved in spite of a damp course being injected into the dining room and the garden room. In August Corinne Bennett was instructed to go ahead with removing the plaster to the right of the chimney in the garden room to try to find out what the problem was. In order to finance this, and other work that was ongoing, money had to be brought in from the Royal Oak Foundation. Fortunately the garden expenses which had been, and still were, considerable, were all being underwritten by the Wallace Funds. In addition to this Barnabas McHenry had suggested to Debo that she put in for a $250,000 endowment for the garden, which he would support. Sadly this very soon came to nothing as he left the administration of the Wallace Foundation. However she had written long, detailed letters to a number of individuals and foundations asking for support for the conservation of the painted wall surfaces and the visitors' centre.

In spite of the financial concerns Debo was able, on 3 September, to write enthusiastically to Mrs Gail Huganir, the editor of *British Heritage* in the United States:

> Since the house has opened Charleston has proved to be a very 'hot' story. The publicity has been just amazing, it has featured in every newspaper and glossy magazine over the last months, and indeed on the front cover of the September issue of *Homes and Gardens*. The American press are just beginning to pick up on it, there have been features in the *New York Times*, *Wall Street Journal* and *The New Yorker*; *Life* magazine are down photographing at this very moment; another feature is about to appear in *People* magazine; and *House and Garden* have been given the first colour exclusive in America, which will run next year. By next year the Laura Ashley publicity will be out too.

Also on the positive side, Piers St Aubyn was able to report, on 5 September, that the total money raised to date was about £750,000 – £170,000 of which had come in 1986.

Achieving all this publicity was taking its toll, particularly on Quentin Bell. He wrote to Debo:

> During the past few days the Bell family have been working extremely hard for Time Life Inc. I suppose that Time Life may get something out of it, we don't, nor I think does Charleston. As you know, this sort of thing has been going on for the past six months and I have lost count of the number of interviews that I have given. I cannot see that these can in any way be related to the donations we have received. Tomorrow morning I have again to go and be photographed at Charleston. I don't think that this process can be of any benefit to Charleston whatsoever.
>
> As you will see, I am fed up, and speaking for myself I should like to say that in future I will give no interviews unless the interviewers have subscribed recently and handsomely to the Trust. Can we inform Alan, Diana and anyone else whom it may concern that QB will speak to no interviewer who has given less that £150 to the Trust and pose for no photographer who has subscribed less than £360? I believe that these decisions are in line with the views expressed at our last Committee meeting.

Although Debo sympathized with him, she did not agree, and sent a personal memorandum to Quentin and Olivier Bell, Vicki Walton, Tina Jeffrey, Diana Reich and Alan Martin.

I have been giving much thought to Quentin's letter of September 8, relating to the press, where he suggests a fee for Charleston of £150 to be interviewed and £360 to be photographed. As he points out, this view was echoed at our last Committee meeting.

I have come to the conclusion this is not good policy. One of the reasons for our success with Charleston is the tremendous support we have had from the press from the very beginning, and I feel this interest should not be deflected but rather should continue to be encouraged. Quentin says he can see no visible fundraising result from all the interviews he has given – but I would suggest the result has been evident at the house, where we have been overwhelmed with visitors and will have some £15,000 in the bank, just when we need it most.

The point is that we must take the long-term view. Our objective has always been to make Charleston known to a wider public. The more articles we can have the better. An article may not necessarily prompt an immediate spate of cheques – but let's be realistic, what makes our task the easier is when, at a later date, an approach is made to a potential donor they have already seen or know something about Charleston.

Therefore I do not think the proposed charges are a good idea – and in the long run counter-productive. Surely what Quentin is really saying – and quite rightly so – is that he has had enough!

We need therefore to call a halt to media activity for the time being and save it until next year when we shall need it.

If there are one or two instances where a visit is set up for a member of the press (e.g. because a reporter is visiting from abroad) then I suggest Quentin is spared. Perhaps Olivier would not mind undertaking the occasional interview – or possibly Richard Shone or Simon Watney.

However, I do feel there is a real need to monitor reporters and the proposed publications very carefully. We do not need (or want) reporters such as Jill Johnston from New York who has no real interest in what Charleston is – but is simply out for her own gain.

I also agree with Richard that we must be very strict with photographers in that they cannot move objects or paintings within the house to 'make a composition', or undertake something that is deemed un-Charlestonian, such as children sitting in the log boxes or the painted bath.

NB: That we have given the first colour feature as an exclusive in America to *House and Garden*, so we need to advise other magazines such as *Connoisseur* who have recently expressed interest.

Although Barnabas McHenry was no longer in charge of the Wallace Foundation funds, Debo had lost no time in getting in touch with Carole Howard, who had been made Vice-President of *Reader's Digest* and was in charge of public relations and communications policy. They met in New York in October and were to meet again in November. Penny Bardel by this time was back in New York, and she too had met with Carole Howard. Later in the year the new director of the Wallace Funds, Arlene Shuler, came to visit Charleston. Debo had also made contact with the Katonah Gallery in up-state New York, which was to play an important part, the following year, in keeping Charleston and its artists in the forefront of people's minds in America.

In London a new promoter and supporter of Charleston and Bloomsbury was the Bloomsbury Workshop. Tony Bradshaw had met Debo at the V&A Symposium in June and had written to her explaining that he and his wife, a bookbinder, were proposing to open a small shop in the courtyard of Pied Bull Court in Bury Place, to sell items associated with the Bloomsbury Group. It opened in December and the press release contained the following description:

> On display, and for sale, will be paintings, drawings and prints by Duncan Grant and Vanessa Bell, as well as some of their associates who exhibited with the 'London Group' in the 1920s and 1930s. There is also a fairly comprehensive stock of books by and about the 'Bloomsbury Group', comprising Proofs, First Editions, Secondhand and New books. A portion of the profits will be donated to the Charleston Trust.

The co-operation between the two organisations was to prove a very happy and successful one.

A hand-written letter to Debo from Lucia Woods Lindley, a very loyal and generous supporter of the Trust, confirmed the entry for the guidebook, acknowledging her sponsorship of the studio. It also contained a message she wanted Debo to pass on to Lisa Anderson of the *Chicago Tribune*, who was writing an article about Charleston. It said: 'Charleston is a celebration of home, hearts and friendship. Much of my energy is given to redressing the inequalities women experience. My involvement with Charleston confirms values, I believe, essential for all, but which few have pursued with such passion. Charleston reminds us of these values, it's a place of sanctuary *and* celebration.' Her message was surely as much about Debo's achievements as about the Bloomsbury world, as she called it.

Good financial news was reported by Debo in a letter to Piers St Aubyn dated 6 December. Paul Mellon had promised $78,750 to meet conversion costs for the visitors' centre; $100,000 had come from the Wallace Funds for the garden; Mrs Margaret McDermott had promised generous funds towards the purchase price of the visitors' centre; and the Robert L. Huffins Jr Foundation $8,500 to sponsor the kitchen. Debo also wrote to Piers about the desirability of forming an editorial committee to oversee the Newsletter. She suggested Olivier Bell, Nigel Nicolson, Simon Watney and Richard Shone. She reported that a number of people felt that the present content and tone did not correctly reflect the views of the Committee as a whole.

Chapter 14

Bloomsbury?

A handful of art critics had always found it easy to sneer at Bloomsbury, and Charleston was inevitably included in this dismissive criticism. Simon Watney, who joined the Committee of the Trust in 1986, wrote a reply to one of these critics. This is part of it:

Friends of Charleston who are regular readers of the *Guardian* will need no introduction to the name of Waldemar Januszczak, the newspaper's leading art critic and gallery reviewer. For almost a decade he has lost no opportunity to abuse and belittle the visual arts of Bloomsbury, a subject to which he returns with relentless and monotonous gusto. This might not matter were there an informed field of art commentary in the British press as a whole, or a body of sustained scholarship in this area in the form of catalogues and monographs. Unfortunately we currently enjoy neither of these luxuries. In this situation Mr Januszczak's opinions acquire the semblance of canonical status through sheer unopposed repetition, allowing him to collapse together the very different objectives and achievements of Duncan Grant, Vanessa Bell and their friends and allies, casually dismissing them all under the name of 'Bloomsbury'. . . .

What is astonishing about all this is the almost total absence of any serious examination of the actual *work* of either Bell or Grant. If there is 'cultism' of any kind it concerns the social and political evaluation of Bloomsbury *as a whole*. However one may estimate the novels of E.M. Forster or Virginia Woolf, it is clear that Bloomsbury represents a tenor of debate – not a coherent stable 'position'. How could it be otherwise in a network of friendship and acquaintance which embraced, at two extremes, Leonard Woolf and Harold Nicolson? Bloomsbury was a dialogue or it was nothing. Only very trivial minds can continue talking about Bloomsbury in the late 1980s as if it were some conscious, intentional and intrinsically coherent entity. . . .

The work of Bell and Grant is regarded in Britain today through a fog of confused and confusing debates concerning characters and personalities rather than actual aesthetic worth. Their work is read *in toto* as if it were a unified sign of something called 'Bloomsbury', rather than an extremely complex, sometimes uneven, contribution to the history of European modernism. It should not therefore surprise us if critics such as Januszczak conclude that the decorations at Charleston are as if 'the Omega Workshops had gone out of control like vegetation in a horror story'.

Debo was rarely roused, but an article in the *New York Times* angered her so much that she felt compelled to respond to it. It was written by Jill Johnston, to whom she had referred in her memorandum about the press. Debo had gone out of her way to be helpful to Johnston after they had met in Dallas. She had sent her copies of lectures and details of the re-creation of the garden. When the article appeared it was snide and point-scoring. Writing to Debo and enclosing a copy of the article, Jill Johnston justified what she had written by saying, 'It has, as you can see, a negative gloss. They wanted all that Soap stuff and I didn't mind myself being "ironic" about the Money and Ruins aspect of Anglo-American relations.' Debo wrote a detailed rationale of her reasons for wanting to preserve Charleston and the ethos behind the Trust, which she sent to the editor of the *New York Times Book Review*:

Yes, we have had enough of Bloomsbury. This is if Bloomsbury is to continue to be portrayed in the sensationalist and slanted manner adopted by Janet Malcolm in her criticism of *Deceived with Kindness* in the October 24 *New York Review* and Jill Johnston's article in the August 24 1986 issue of the *New York Times Book Review*. Surely this is torpid reporting, we are not being presented with anything we do not already know, but rather would it not be more constructive to concentrate upon the real achievements to which these brilliant and witty individuals directed their lives and energies?

Ought we not be more considerate (or should I here more aptly use the word 'serious') and aware of our responsibilities? Each generation has to carry the legacy of its forebears. Should we not allow the present generation (and their children) the freedom to be and to express their own individuality, rather than hinder them with ghosts of the past and place them in a straitjacket of our own fetish?

Perhaps I may reply to Jill Johnston's article? In the first place, one may equate Bloomsbury with Charleston, but it is not strictly accurate. Of course, one is not saying Bloomsbury is not a part of Charleston – but the main point is that Charleston represents a far wider circle, and one could even go one step further and say that Charleston was a refuge from Bloomsbury.

May I also correct Ms Johnston's statement that 'Part of the effort to preserve Charleston has centred on tapping the endless appetite for Bloomsbury among Americans'. I have been the moving force and co-ordinator of the project. The reason for my having based any activities in America has been that for the last fifteen years I have been more in the American continent than anywhere else. Far from tapping 'Bloomsburiana', it is not unreasonable to expect events to occur where I may happen to be.

I have always based my appeal for Charleston upon the merits of the case, not necessarily based upon the achievements of the artists Vanessa Bell and Duncan Grant, but more in terms of its context with regard to a certain moment in the history of British art and the cultural and literary heritage of our English language. Charleston's significance lies in its standing as a personal and historic document of the twentieth century. By its example I have also wanted to draw attention to the fact that there is a need for greater awareness to preserve aspects of our modern day heritage as well as the past. The more so since the mode of present day living has developed more in terms of an intimate human scale, rather than the grand stately edifices of a foregone era; consequently modern environments are more vulnerable to wear and tear, alteration and changes of ownership.

Ms Johnston has not presented us with a complete picture of the aims and objectives of the Charleston Trust, and perhaps I may expand a little upon this theme. In the first instance the Trust, a registered charity in England, has two purposes. The first is to restore and preserve Charleston in perpetuity for the benefit of future generations.

However, restoration does not simply relate to bricks and mortar. Charleston was a nucleus for intellectual discourse, the sparring of wit and creativity. The point of saving this essential element should not become fossilised – rather the exchange of ideas and the intellectual process should continue to evolve. Thus the second objective of the Charleston Trust has been to stimulate an imaginative programme devoted to the art and literature of the twentieth century, and this endeavour will come into far greater play as we have more time to devote to this area, once our responsibilities are accomplished in other areas relating to the house. It is essential not to confuse the two objectives.

The programme of events described in Dallas this March is part of a series that have been organised over the last six years in conjunction with the Victoria and Albert Museum, London, and the Metropolitan Museum and Cooper-Hewitt in New York. There was in fact a very good reason for us to be in Texas, which Ms Johnston omitted to mention. One of the most comprehensive archives relating to Virginia and Leonard Woolf, Vanessa Bell, Roger Fry, David Garnett, Maynard Keynes, Lytton Strachey, Dora Carrington, Lady Ottoline Morrell, T.S. Eliot, E.M. Forster, D.H. Lawrence, and Bertrand Russell and this rich period of twentieth-century literature and letters is housed at the Harry Ransom Humanities Research Centre, University of Texas at Austin. These archives were extensively used in the display of 'The Handprinted Books of Leonard and Virginia Woolf at the Hogarth Press, 1917–1932' organised by the Fine Arts Division at the Dallas Public Library, and was the exhibition central to our series of events.

Furthermore, it was not emphasised that while some sections of the Dallas programme related directly to Charleston, there was a special day set aside where participants were invited to present their own material – the whole point of establishing a forum related to twentieth-century art and literature is that new ideas and new material should be encouraged and shared. Reference was made to Dr Barbara Wedgwood and her excellent talk on the 'Tempestuous Victorians: The Romantic Friendship of Robert Browning and Julia Wedgwood', a subject on which she is a great authority. No mention was made of the other participants, such as Professor Frederic Turner, whose lecture subsequently received a literary nomination and was published in the summer issue of *Missouri Review.*

What we have endeavoured to present from the outset has been a series of programmes of a very high calibre, drawing upon a varied and distinguished circle of art and literary figures. In a short time we have built a reputation for a series that has already met with widespread acclaim and recognition and has come to attract a following from all over the United States and Canada.

Far from a 'Ruin', I would venture to suggest that Charleston has become a very lively and stimulating platform. Were this not the case, our events at Dallas, for example, would not have attracted participants of the stature they did, nor would they have had the support of no less than five hundred institutions, some of which may be considered among the most significant in the country. In the light of which, I wonder whether Ms Johnston's comments were altogether fair to the participants who gave their time so freely and generously, or to Dallas, a city that has always welcomed new ideas.

Chapter 15

Changes

The publicity which followed the opening continued for the rest of 1986 and into 1987. This meant there was an obvious danger the public would think the job was done and no more support or money was needed, which was very far from the truth. There was also the unresolved problem of replacing the chairman. On 25 January Debo wrote to Robert Skidelsky asking him if he would consider accepting the chairmanship. Although he was Professor of International Studies at the University of Warwick, he had taken on the lease of Tilton, the former house of Maynard Keynes, whose official biography he was in the process of writing. The second volume had been published in 1986 and the third was yet to be written. She had talked to him at a party given by her cousin at Firle Place on Christmas Eve. Her letter spelled out the problems that still had to be solved at Charleston, but assured him that the position would not be an onerous one. Two days later he replied to say that in principle he would be happy to serve as chairman. He was a little apprehensive about the amount of work it might involve and about the possible expectation of financial feats similar to those of Maynard Keynes, the previous occupant of Tilton. Debo replied from America, suggesting that they meet to talk about what would be involved when she returned at the end of February.

Further changes were to follow. On 28 January Nigel Nicolson wrote to Debo to say that he wanted to retire from the Committee at the AGM. On 18 March Debo wrote to him to say that she too intended to resign at the AGM. While she had been in America during February Nigel Nicolson had met and written to Hugh Lee about the Newsletter, which had been an unsolved problem for some while. In spite of this, little had been resolved. Debo felt strongly that the Committee should have editorial control of the Newsletter but this had not been agreed to at the last meeting. She elaborated on her reasons for resigning in a letter to Robert Skidelsky on 31 March. She began by expressing her delight that he had agreed to take on the chairmanship and went on:

> I confess I feel somewhat of a fraud writing to you now to tell you that I have notified the Committee I shall be retiring at the AGM on June 27.
> This puts me – and you – in a difficult position because of course I gave you my word

that a great deal of the administrative side of the Committee would fall upon my shoulders, leaving you with the freedom to complete your biography of Keynes.

The reason for my departure is two-fold. In the first instance, I believe I told you I am in the process of opening a gallery in Bond Street. Since I saw you, I have had to make rather more commitments in this regard than I had anticipated, putting me under greater pressures.... This is coupled with a recent Committee decision regarding policy for the Newsletter, with which, I am afraid I am not in accord....

In effect what I propose is to continue as a Trustee. As I have been the 'link' person regarding so many aspects, without a certain amount of liaison I feel a large number of contacts built up over the years will be lost. Also, as I mentioned to you, there are various potentially large donors that I have been nurturing; clearly I shall see these through – I hope to a successful conclusion. The point is that I have no intention of leaving either the Committee or you 'in the lurch', and, of course, I shall support you in any way I am able.

Nigel Nicolson asked me whether I had any ideas as to the best person to take over my position as Secretary to the Committee. I replied that I thought Alan Martin would be a good choice. Apart from the family, Alan is the person I have worked most closely with on this Committee over the years, so he really does know everything inside out!

... Turning to different matters, our AGM is set for Saturday, June 27, at the Corn Exchange in Brighton, which I do hope is a convenient date for you. We propose to arrange a lunch for Friends, followed by the AGM itself at 2.30. After we have dealt with the formalities, it has become our practice to turn the platform over to a guest to provide us with a talk. Speakers in the past have included Quentin, Pamela Diamond and Frances Partridge and this formula has made for a most enjoyable day.

We wondered whether you might like to give the talk this year, perhaps on the subject of Charleston and Tilton, very much along the lines of your article that appeared in Newsletter No.6. I know it would be well received and a great success!

Her letter and the news it contained, which she later sent to the members of the Committee, caused great consternation. Nigel Nicolson and Robert Skidelsky tried desperately to get her to change her mind, but without success. Robert Skidelsky wrote to Nigel Nicolson reserving his position until he had more information about the financial state of the Trust and its constitution. Nigel Nicolson then completed the circle by communicating with Debo. She confirmed that she and Robert Skidelsky had met and that he had said he would only take on the chairmanship if she took a 'leave of absence' for a year from the Committee. This she refused to do. But as she had no wish to leave the Trust in the lurch, she hoped that by remaining in the background she could assist with the handing over process, and from time to time perhaps the opportunity would arise for her to direct the odd donor in Charleston's way.

In spite of the somewhat precarious state of the Trust's finances, Robert Skidelsky did agree to take on the chairmanship, to the great relief and delight of everyone. He also agreed to give the talk. The resignations and handovers would not of course take effect until the AGM on 27 June. This was held in the Corn Exchange in Brighton and attended by a large number of Friends. Nigel Nicolson, as acting chairman, presented the Annual Report. He marvelled at the achievements so far, saying, 'Charleston is not over-restored but revitalized.' He went on to pay tribute to the generosity of Mrs Lila Acheson Wallace and the skill of Sir Peter Shepheard and Mark Divall in restoring the garden. He thanked Vicki Walton and Tina Jeffrey for their untiring work in dealing with the 12,000 people who visited the house between June and October in 1986. He reported that, although £800,000 had been raised, there were still some major things to be done which needed funds. He also announced his retirement as acting chairman and Deborah Gage's as honorary secretary. He introduced Professor Robert Skidelsky, his successor designate, and Alan Martin who was to be the new honorary secretary. Virginia Bell, Quentin's daughter, was elected vice-chairman. Debo was unable to attend the AGM and had specifically stated that fulsome thanks to her would not be appropriate. Nigel Nicolson did, however, express everyone's gratitude and admiration and ended by quoting from Alexander Pope's poem:

> When all the world conspires to praise her,
> The woman's deaf, and does not hear.

This was greeted by prolonged applause.

A warm tribute was also paid to Nigel Nicolson for all the work he had done for the Trust since its early days. He may have opposed Debo on a number of things, especially the decorated wall surfaces, but his contribution to the whole programme had been immense, not simply as vice- and then acting chairman, but as a chairman and speaker at the symposia in Britain and particularly in America. He was an excellent chairman and an amusing and interesting speaker on many subjects. His contribution to raising the profile of the Trust was invaluable.

Clearly the most pressing need before and after the AGM was to find sources of continuing funds. Money had been promised for the visitors' centre and the decorated wall surfaces but more was needed. Debo followed up her meeting with Carole Howard of *Reader's Digest* in New York at the end of 1986 with a letter on 28 March. She had been rung by Anthony Masterson-Smith, who represented *Reader's Digest* in London, asking if he and Carole Howard could come down to Charleston on 14 July. She wrote enthusiastically to say that she was delighted and would look forward to welcoming them both most warmly.

Writing to Robert Skidelsky, asking him to put 14 July in his diary, she elaborated on the relationship between *Reader's Digest* and Charleston. In another letter, dated

9 July, she expressed her pleasure that he and his wife could come to lunch on 14 July, together with Lawrence Gowing, a charming and eminent artist, teacher and curator. Elaborating on Carole Howard she wrote: 'What is absolutely essential with Carole is to spark her off with the idea that Charleston really does have great potential from the fact that it captures everyone's imagination – and this in turn provides great potential for Carole to make something of *Reader's Digest*'s association with the project.'

The day after the lunch she wrote to Robert Skidelsky: 'The day appears to have been a great success. Carole Howard was both captivated and inspired by the house and the garden – so let's hope we can reap rewards in due course.' Carole Howard wrote on 20 July:

Many thanks for all the planning you did to make our day in Charleston so very memorable. The beautiful gardens and house lived up to the wonderful advance billing you had given them. And the company and conversation around Vanessa's dining room table made for a very special day indeed ... Many thanks for your warm hospitality – a lovely example of that famous English charm.

Lunch had been prepared by Vicki in the kitchen. They had sat and ate at the table used every day by the family, which had clearly made her feel very much part of the house and its future, and involved her in its conservation. Although the hoped-for endowment for the garden did not materialize, funds were forthcoming for the visitors' centre.

Her letter also referred to the Katonah/*Reader's Digest* symposium in October. The Katonah Gallery, in up-state New York, was established in 1953 as 'a teaching museum, presenting exhibitions of art education programs of the highest quality in the setting of a small museum'. It was situated quite near to the headquarters of *Reader's Digest* in Chappaqua, where an auditorium had been built in memory of DeWitt Wallace, its co-founder. Debo had conceived the idea of an exhibition at the gallery of the twenty-two Bloomsbury-related paintings and lithographs which had been bought by the Wallaces and were now part of the *Reader's Digest* collection. They represented the largest collection of Bloomsbury paintings in America at the time. The exhibition would run in conjunction with a one day symposium at the newly opened auditorium. She had secured the services of Dr Susan Casteras, the curator of Paul Mellon's Museum at Yale, to curate the exhibition. After lengthy correspondence with Myrna Clyman, the Project Director at the Katonah Gallery, the dates for the exhibition, called *Bloomsbury Artists at Charleston*, were fixed for 23 August to 25 October; the symposium was to take place on 10 October. The speakers for the symposium were: Carole Howard and Frances N. Chaves, who would give welcoming remarks; Dr S.P. Rosenbaum on 'Bloomsbury and the Common

Reader'; Dr Susan Casteras on 'Vanessa Bell and the Portrait of an Era'; Deborah Gage on 'The Restoration of Charleston Farmhouse'; Sir Peter Shepheard on 'Bloomsbury Gardens'; and Nigel Nicolson on 'Bloomsbury The Myth and the Reality'. The film *Duncan Grant at Charleston* was also to be shown.

Bloomsbury Artists at Charleston

Paintings from the Reader's Digest Collection

August 23 - October 25, 1987

The Katonah Gallery
Katonah, New York

Programme for the Katonah Gallery's exhibition of Bloomsbury paintings showing
The Dining Room Window, Charleston, by Vanessa Bell, on the cover

Press releases were sent out and a huge amount of publicity was generated. Nearly 400 people came to the symposium and a great many newspaper and journal articles resulted from it. Two weeks later, Debo wrote to Robert Skidelsky about it, and about publicity and fundraising in general.

I can only pass on to you my thoughts and experience with regard to fundraising, especially in relation to the United States. I had based my strategy upon what had been passed on to me by way of one or two highly successful professional fundraisers. They told me, at the end of the day, what it comes down to is having a handful of really good supporters. Do not accept the fact that they will give once, but continue to keep them involved and interested in the ongoing aspects of the project.

As I mentioned to you, what Americans understand and will encourage is enterprise. This is the course I have followed and indeed discovered that by maintaining an active programme I have kept my key donors involved and they have subsequently given time and time again. Examples include Lucia Woods Lindley, Margaret McDermott, *Reader's Digest* – and now we have Paul Mellon coming back with more funding.

I am enclosing details of the typical kind of event I have instigated – the exhibition and symposium at Katonah. In the first instance the publicity has been extraordinary… there is a huge file of clippings and articles that have appeared in the American press. This helps make Charleston itself known to a wider audience, which in turn makes the task of fundraising in the United States easier … More importantly this single event has made our two major donors extremely happy and the more involved and interested in our project – i.e. *Reader's Digest* and Paul Mellon.

I think you will find it is very much to Charleston's long-term advantage and I hope you will be able to continue to work and think along these lines in future. Not only from an immediate fundraising standpoint but also this kind of function and role does fulfil the second objective of the Trust. As a result of Katonah, I think you can look to greater commitment on the part of *Reader's Digest* in future.

Chapter 16

Back at the House

The main preoccupation during 1987 – apart from the continuing problem of rising damp – was the provision of the visitors' centre. The proposal was to buy and convert the block of farm buildings opposite the house, on the other side of the drive. They consisted of a small barn and a row of cowsheds ending in a dairy. The barn and the cowsheds would convert into a shop with a ticket counter, a studio/workroom and a waiting area for exhibitions and the showing of the film *Duncan Grant at Charleston*. A bull pen in the yard at the back would be built up and roofed to provide office space, a kitchen and storage. The purchase of the buildings was delayed by the insistence of the trustees of the Firle Estate that a restrictive clause should be included preventing the use of the building to raise a mortgage. However, before the building actually belonged to the Trust, permission was given to use the dairy to develop toilet facilities. The invasion of the house by many thousands of people had severely strained the very limited facilities in the house itself.

In April Debo contacted Douglas Woolf at the Fulham Pottery, which he ran in partnership with Quentin Bell, to suggest they provide sponsorship of £10,000 towards the development of the shop, on the understanding that it would provide an outlet for their pottery. She also suggested looking into the possibility of a mail-order business to provide an income when the shop was not open. He agreed to provide £7,500, which might be increased to £10,000 in future, as long as the centre remained in being for a minimum of five years. This arrangement closely involved Vicki Walton. Quentin had written to Debo about this and the possible involvement of the Fulham Pottery in January of 1987. Vicki had for some years now been Quentin's assistant and an apprentice at the Pottery; but her time had been more and more swallowed up by Charleston, to the extent that she was overstretched and had little spare time for pottery. He wrote:

> I think it must be understood she is an artist, that her real passion is for ceramic work and that having been a most useful apprentice for me, she is now becoming a qualified worker in her own right with the beginnings of a good reputation.
>
> I had hoped that she might be sufficiently well established by the time that I have to leave the scene to be able to set up a pottery of her own in Charleston thus, in effect,

bringing the pottery back to Charleston but with the added advantage of having a retail outlet at her door. To this end, I am leaving her all the equipment in my pottery and I had proposed to suggest to Douglas Woolf that he contribute to the provision of a shop and its ancillary services at Charleston so that he would have a permanent stake in the success of Charleston, its pottery and its shop. The prospect of doing this now begins to look rather dim. Vicki was hardly able to meet the immediate demands of Christmas and still has, I believe, a number of commissions which she simply does not have time to finish because as a potter she is being extinguished. I am sure that this is something that you do not want to happen either for her sake or for Charleston's, and I believe that her devotion to her art is such that if she had to choose between Charleston and continuing as a studio potter, she would leave Charleston.

When Robert Skidelsky became chairman her situation was greatly improved by giving her an assistant and increasing her salary. Nevertheless the calls upon her were still manifold and she was rightly described as 'the cement that holds everything together both in and out'.

The disabled, gents' and ladies' toilets, decorated with tiles by Quentin Bell

Meanwhile the drains and plumbing for the toilet facilities in the visitors' centre were being installed. By the end of July sufficient work had been done for Virginia Bell to write to Lucinda Lambton – the well known photographer, broadcaster and author of *Temples of Convenience* – asking her if she would come and perform an opening ceremony. She wrote that the gents', ladies' and disabled toilets were to be 'decorated in original, inimitable style with splendid coloured ceramic tiles made by my father Quentin Bell: the highlight will be naked ladies in the Gents, though the other loos will have slightly more tasteful decorative schemes.'

The work on the visitors' centre had been divided into three phases; the first had now been completed. In October the buildings were finally bought for £25,000 and the work of converting the rest of them started. The funding was provided by the Royal Oak Foundation and Philip Bottomley, who had overall responsibility for the work, was given the go-ahead to start on the second phase, which involved the conversion of the barn and cowsheds. By this time it had been decided that the office should be housed in the cowsheds rather than in the bull pen, which would now only provide a kitchen and storage space. In the end the bull pen was not incorporated and a small kitchen was created at the back of the office space in the cowsheds. By the end of December almost all the building work had been completed. There was a certain amount of disquiet about the quality of the work and the cheeseparing that had occurred; but it seemed too late to do anything about this.

When Debo resigned from the Committee finances became more of a problem. Vicki Walton had valiantly kept all the housekeeping accounts and Piers St Aubyn had been an extremely conscientious and willing bookkeeper; but Debo had controlled all donations and authorized all payments and borrowings. Alan Martin did not want to do this, nor did Robert Skidelsky. Also, with the opening of the house and the shop, the whole thing had become much more complicated. It was therefore suggested that a professional should be brought in to oversee all financial matters. David Clark had been the accountant for a while and Robert Skidelsky wrote to Piers St Aubyn asking for his agreement that David should take over the job of treasurer as well. As Piers's wife was extremely ill at the time he readily agreed to this. It meant that the finances could be put on an improved system, strictly dividing capital from current accounts. Signing powers would be in the hands of David Clark with Robert Skidelsky and Virginia Bell as co-signatories. By the middle of December all this had been settled and a trading company had been set up to deal with the sales from the shop, which had to be kept separate so as not to endanger the charitable status of the Trust.

The major unresolved problem in the house itself was the rising damp and the completion of the decorated wall surfaces. Debo had contacted Joan Davidson, the President of the J.M. Kaplan Fund in New York, in the hope that they might sponsor this. She replied saying that she would like to visit Charleston along with a board member of the British American Arts Association. Writing to Robert Skidelsky about this Debo explained that it was very unusual for the Kaplan Foundation or any member of the family to sponsor anything outside New York. It seemed Joan David-son had been intrigued by the way the campaign had been mounted in America rather than by an interest in Bloomsbury itself. Her visit to Charleston, like that of Carole Howard, included lunch eaten at Vanessa Bell's table in the dining room. The result was a cheque for $9,000. This, together with an additional grant from English Her-itage of £10,000, allowed the work to start up again. The damp in the garden room had been cured but there were cracks in the plaster that needed attention. The damp in the dining room was still a problem and in October Debo wrote to Corinne Ben-nett to say that it was clearly going to be necessary to remove all the plaster from one wall and start again with a fresh damp-proof render. This clearly meant that there was no possibility of rehanging the paper before April and it would almost certainly be sensible to delay it until the winter of 1988. In December she wrote to Robert Skidel-sky to tell him that she had met Phillip Stevens to sort out arrangements for the next stage of the work. Heather Wood, who had overseen all the work so far, had a new job at Brighton Pavilion, which might slow the work down, but this seemed a small price to pay to maintain continuity.

Chapter 17

More Changes

At the beginning of 1988 there were again financial worries, but they did not involve the finishing of the visitors' centre. Funds were being held by the Royal Oak Foundation in New York and Olivier and Virginia Bell had taken over the development of the interior. Writing in the Newsletter at the end of the season Tina Jeffrey described the visitors' centre:

> The move across the lane to the cowshed, sensitively converted for use as a visitors' centre, shop and gallery, has meant greater tranquillity in the house and more discreet assembling of visitors on guided visit days. There have been many appreciative comments about the new premises and the good things that one can buy there – ceramics by Quentin Bell, Vicki Walton, Sophie McCarthy and Philip Sutton and from the Fulham Pottery; textiles by Cressida Bell; decorated lampshades and a good range of books and postcards. People appear to have stocked their entire gardens from the range of plants and garden pots on sale this year.

Before the opening, in 1988, the garden room had been distempered grey, the over-mantel replaced, the furniture and pictures put back where they had been and new curtains hung. It was decided to do this before the decorated wall surfaces could be returned because the room had played such an important part in the lives of the people who lived there.

Clearly nobody had realized quite how much Debo had done. Her leaving had left a huge administrative gap. Robert Skidelsky wrote to her on 28 May deploring the fact that, while they clearly needed a full-time director, there did not seem to be enough funds to allow this. By August it had become apparent this must happen. Christopher Naylor was appointed, initially for a two-year period, to start in September. With a colleague, he had been instrumental in founding the Almeida Theatre in Islington and currently was Director of Appeals at the Rainer Foundation. Robert Skidelsky believed that the future of the Trust lay in developing Charleston Enterprises, which would need a director who 'thought big'. He felt Christopher Naylor fitted this description.

Also in August, Vicki and Cyril announced they would be leaving at the end of October to go and live in Wales, where she would establish her own pottery. This would leave another huge gap. It was decided that Mark Divall would take over the flat and so become the resident caretaker. Geraldine Guest would become curator. But Vicki had been so much more than caretaker and curator. Debo masterminded the restoration but Vicki was the linchpin. If she had not been in the house it could not have succeeded. Debo and she talked on the phone every night and she kept everything and everyone going. The following is a part of what Millie Collins wrote in the Newsletter:

On Sunday, October 30, Charleston was the setting for a farewell party for Vicki Walton. From the very beginning of the restoration Vicki has been more involved with its incredibly complex problems than anyone else and has borne the brunt of the day-to-day organization.

…There were early Open Days for Friends of Charleston which involved Vicki in clearing up, cleaning, catering and gardening to ensure that everything looked as well as it could on the day; only for everything to be put away again as work on the fabric continued. As the opening of the first season drew near, more and more devolved onto Vicki. During all these years she also worked as Quentin's pottery assistant four mornings a week, and developed her own pottery technique as well.

The Young Lady of Firle, likened to Vicki Walton,
the caretaker and curator of Charleston from 1981–87

Vicki remained cheerful, warm and generous. Her smile and manner attracted many people to work for Charleston. To those of us privileged to know her, her friendship was delightful, spontaneous and caring. Some Friends and visitors may have known her only as a name at the end of a list of staff, but they will have experienced her presence in every room in the shape of vases overflowing with flowers and in the presentation of the house, reflecting her love of Charleston and her sense of the spirit of its former occupants.

After nearly a decade of whole-hearted devotion to Charleston Vicki is now moving to Wales to set up her own pottery and home with Cyril. On the last day of the 1988 season members of the Committee, staff, guides and many personal friends gathered for a lunch party to pay tribute. Quentin spoke of his own and our sense of loss. He said he had three things to say: damn, because she is going; love and gratitude for all she had been to him, his family and Charleston; and good luck for the future.

Deborah Gage spoke of her own and our debt to Vicki as the hub around which for many years the endeavours of the restoration and the Committee had revolved. After presenting Vicki with a cheque to help her set up her new pottery Debo, fancying a resemblance, quoted a limerick by Edward Lear:

There was a Young Lady of Firle, whose hair was addicted to curl
It curled up a Tree, and all over the Sea,
That expansive Young Lady of Firle.

Vicki your smile and warmth of heart are expansive indeed.
We are diminished by your going.

In October and November of 1987 Debo had written to Robert Skidelsky about the importance of keeping alive the seminars, which had played such an important part in raising interest in Charleston in America. She suggested the original format should be adapted to be more of a study week – or summer school as it later became – which should take place in England. The first, very grandiose one, had been abandoned for a number of reasons. But the involvement of the Savoy Group, Victoria Smith of Omega Limited, tour operators in England and the Royal Oak Foundation was revived in 1988. A week-long seminar was arranged, based largely at West Dean College in West Sussex. All travel arrangements were made in conjunction with a New York firm and the fee of $3,000 was all-inclusive.

The programme was arranged entirely by the Charleston Trust, something Debo felt was most important. The first two nights were spent in London at the Savoy Hotel. On the first evening there was a reception at the hotel where personalities associated with Charleston were present. The following day included visits to the Tate and the Courtauld Institute, with illustrated lectures by Simon Watney and Richard Shone. Lunch was in the Whistler Restaurant at the Tate. The following morning they went by coach to West Dean, stopping at the Spread Eagle in Midhurst for lunch. In the evening Lord Norwich gave a talk on the heritage of England and introduced the first part of the film *The Treasure Houses of Britain*. After dinner the second part was shown. On the third day Frances Spalding gave a talk about Vanessa Bell and they were then driven to Charleston to look at the house and garden and have lunch. After lunch they went to see the murals in Berwick church. In the evening they had dinner back at West Dean and saw the last part of *The Treasure Houses of Britain.*

The fourth day was devoted to Vita Sackville-West. Victoria Glendinning, her biographer, talked about her and they were then driven to Sissinghurst to be welcomed by Nigel Nicolson and visit the garden. Lunch was served in the beautiful, original barn. In the evening they were allowed to relax! The next day Virginia Woolf was the central subject. Michael Holroyd talked about her and they were driven to Monks House. During the day they were shown the film of *To the Lighthouse* and in the evening Patrick Garland put on a dramatization of *A Room of One's Own.*

On the final day Judith Collins, an art historian, gave a talk on the Omega Workshops. They were then invited to walk in the gardens at West Dean and visit their workshops, where a variety of courses are held. The college is famous for its weaving of designs by Henry Moore and John Piper. In the afternoon there was a voluntary visit to Chichester cathedral. A gala dinner in the evening was held at Goodwood House, the home of the Duke of Richmond since 1697, at the end of which Margaret Drabble talked about 'Landscape and Literature'. The following morning they departed for New York. Although there were few takers for this first one its popularity grew and grew.

Chapter 18

Completing the Garden Room and Dining Room

On 5 November 1989 Debo announced her resignation as a trustee. Her own business was demanding her full attention and she no longer had the time to devote to Charleston. She also felt the job she had set out to do had been completed. The future was for others. She had made all the necessary arrangements for replacing the decorated wall surfaces in the garden room and the dining room, which was the final thing she had promised to do. From the start they had been both problematic and controversial. They remained so until the end. The bold pattern on its black background in the dining room was designed, in 1939, by Duncan Grant and executed by him and Quentin, almost certainly as a distraction from the mounting threat of war. The paisley pattern in the garden room was Vanessa Bell's design and executed by her and Duncan Grant in 1945. On its pale grey background it was peaceful and almost old fashioned. Both had been painted directly onto whatever was on the walls before – paper or just plaster – or onto cheap lining paper.

Because of the continuing problem of damp in the dining room the paper in the garden room was the first to be replaced. The original hand-stirred grey distemper was made up of powdered pigment and rabbit-skin size, mixed with chalk, to give it body. Two or three coats of this had been applied over the existing wallpaper or poor-quality brown lining paper. The darker grey paisley shape was created by sponging it through a paper stencil, then the white flowers were stencilled and, finally, the yellow spots were painted on. When the paint dried the chalk gave it a bloom reminiscent of fresco paintings. Although the finish was effective it was far from stable. The lack of preparation, the lack of binding in the distemper, the poor quality of the materials, the acidity of the paper, all made the surface extremely fragile, with a tendency to flake.

By the time the paper was removed from the walls in 1981 the decorations had been in place for thirty-six years. The room was heated by an open coal fire; it was used daily by numbers of people, many of whom smoked; sun came through the window to the east; and, although the French windows faced north, they would, when open, have allowed flies and other insects to come in. Pictures hung on all the walls, creating marks; other, much worse marks were caused by damp. In the last years of Duncan Grant's life the whole house had become damp and derelict, and in the garden room this had caused the brown from the lining paper to stain the design. By 1981, mould had encroached on all the layers of paper. When they were removed from the walls by Phillip Stevens's team, they were put on special 8- by 4-foot pallets, which had feet so they could be stacked one above another. They were then stored at one of Bonhams' warehouses in London until funds were available for their conservation.

Everything not returned to Charleston in 1986 was stored at Phillip Stevens's studio until 1988, when further funds became available. In November 1988 all these items came to Charleston. These included, not only the papers from the garden room and the dining room, but a dozen smaller items. Further treatment was to be done by Heather Wood, who had recently moved to Sussex. She had worked in Phillip Stevens's studio since 1985 and, with others, had been responsible for all the work done so far on the decorated wall surfaces. They were transported on their pallets and left to acclimatize in the studio at Charleston. Meanwhile, in December, the garden room was cleared of furniture and the picture rails and radiator removed. The grey distemper was washed from the walls, which were painted with glue size. They were then lined with Japanese Bankoshi paper using a wheat starch paste mixed with 5%

PVA. Next came a 'release layer' of 115 cm wide, 35% cotton and 65% polyester. This was fixed with the same adhesive and was a precautionary measure in case the panels needed to be removed at a future date. Finally came another layer of Japanese paper, this time using wheat starch paste.

During December Heather Wood also lined and repaired the ten sections which had not been finished in Phillip Stevens's studio. All the sections were once more consolidated with varying concentrations of Klucel G and L in isopropyl alcohol. In January Heather was joined by Monika Gast, who came specially from Germany to help with the

Garden room paper stained by the lining paper

Replacing the paper in the garden room

rehanging. She was an expert at speedy pasting and hanging, which was essential to avoid the paste dampening and destabilizing or staining the surface. In the last week of January drops of wallpaper were hung on the radiator wall and on the wall to the left of the fireplace. Each section was pasted with very dry sodium alginate and arrowroot and hung and dried as quickly as possible before the paint layers were disturbed. During the last week of February further drops were hung on the north wall and on the top half of the one to the right of the fireplace. As the walls had been replastered – some a number of times – the dimensions had altered slightly. This meant a certain amount of trimming and infilling was necessary. Small areas were repaired with Tenjugo facing tissue, which was then toned in using Rowneys artists' pastels, compressed charcoal, Louvre soft pastel, Sennelier pastels and Winsor and Newton watercolours. Once the viable drops had been hung, they were faced with the problem of completing the remaining areas with facsimiles. These included the whole of the window wall, the bottom of the wall to the right of the fireplace and some of the border. In addition to this a considerable amount of retouching was needed in damaged areas of the originals. All this was done by Wilma Harper and Susannah Penrose.

The distemper they used for this was made up of Cornelissen pigments, Whiting and concentrated gelatine – two thirds of a sachet of gelatine to one pint of water. The grey ground coat was a mix of Whiting, Raw Umber, Ivory Black, Yellow Ochre, Venetian Red, Chrome Oxide, and a dash of Cadmium Yellow. This was applied in three layers: two ground coats mixed with size, finished with a light wash. Across the window wall the grey background had to change from dark to lighter to match the differing shades at either end. Also, missing areas of paper on the walls had to be filled to disguise the joins between the original and the facsimile.

The dark grey paisley design was sponged through a paper stencil and was a mix of Ivory Black, Raw Umber, Burnt Umber, Yellow Ochre and Whiting. The white flowers were stencilled on using Whiting, Raw Umber and Yellow Ochre. Finally the yellow spots were painted on using Cadmium Yellow Light and Raw Umber. The pattern on the border was painted using Whiting, Lamp Black and Raw Umber. This was very difficult to do without allowing paint to dribble onto the wall below. Once the facsimiles had been completed on the window wall and the one to the right of the fireplace, they were distressed to harmonize with the original. Because of the fragility of these wall decorations it was reluctantly decided that a Perspex panel should be fixed to protect the most vulnerable area, just inside the door. In May 1989 everything was replaced in the garden room and it was once more opened to the public.

The damp problem in the dining room continued to be unsolved. Both the south wall and the east wall, surrounding the fireplace, were given further remedial treatment a number of times. Finally, at the end of 1991, they were dry enough for work to begin. An unexpected problem immediately arose. In 1984 some of the walls had been papered using an adhesive with an excessive amount of PVA, which proved very hard to remove. In 1985, Angelica Garnett had painted the whole room black without sizing the exposed plaster and the black distemper had sunk deep into it and had to be scrubbed

Stenciling the facsimiles in the garden room

off. All this took time, but once these two things had been done, any holes or cracks in the plaster were made good and the walls were ready to be lined.

This was done with an acid-free lining paper using a wheat starch paste with 5% PVA . On the walls, where dampness had been such an intractable problem, a small amount of formaldehyde was added to the paste to reduce the risk of mould appearing in the future. The release lining of cotton and polyester came next and finally a Heritage wood-free 120 gsm paper. Before the original drops could be rehung a number of measurements and adjustments had to be made. The window in the east wall had been replaced and a sill added; the new skirting boards were 2 inches deeper, which meant reducing the length of the drop so the complete design appeared below the picture rail. As in the garden room the replastering had slightly altered the shape and size of all the walls.

The north wall, to the left of the door from the hall, was the first to be rehung. The picture rail was measured and marked out to ensure the border would fit above it. The top section of the first drop was put face down on blotters. A thin paste of sodium alginate was then applied to the area of the wall to be hung. The back of the section was pasted with a thicker solution, turned over and quickly applied to the wall. It was then smoothed down with blotters to remove any air bubbles. This process was

repeated for all the other sections. The lower area of drops four and five proved very problematic because earlier damp had made the paint film very weak. As the paste dried, the adhesion of the thick black distemper to an underlying surface of old distemper was broken, and there was danger of flaking and crazing of the paint layer. This had always been a problem and had necessitated extensive fixing and consolidation, but there was always a danger that it would not be successful. Fortunately it only really occurred in this one area. Using a carrier of isopropyl alcohol, a strong gelatine solution was inserted between and under lifting flakes and pressure applied until

Section of the original decoration in the dining room

Painting in the lines in the dining room

they readhered. In order to protect this very vulnerable surface, a Perspex panel was fixed just inside the door, as in the garden room.

The east wall was hung in the same manner. The paint film on these drops had been damaged and was much thinner, which had made it easier to consolidate, leaving only a few areas of flaking and lifting. These were treated in the same way as on the north wall. Because of the changes caused by the replastering, infill repairs had to be made along the top of the north wall and round the window on the east wall. Moreover, when the sections had been removed, a small amount of paper had been lost along all the edges. These were filled either with coloured Canson paper or with distemper to close the gap and disguise the joins. Then a considerable amount of retouching was done on both walls.

Most of design on the south and west walls had been painted directly onto plaster. They were the two walls that had repeatedly been treated for damp. This meant the design had to be facsimiled by Wilma Harper and Susannah Penrose. The distemper they used was once more made up of Cornelissen pigments and concentrated

The dining room when it was completed in 1992

gelatine – two-thirds of a sachet of gelatine to one pint of water. The black ground coat was a mix of Ivory Black and Yellow Ochre. This was applied in three layers: two ground coats mixed with size, finished with a light wash. The grey squares and the circles for the missing areas of the border were sponged through paper stencils, using Ivory Black and Whiting. The yellow chevrons and lines were then painted on using Yellow Ochre, Raw Umber, Cadmium Yellow and Whiting. These walls, as in the garden room, were distressed to make them blend in with the original on the other two walls. The picture rails were put back, the furniture returned and the pictures and curtains hung. The room was ready for the opening in April 1992 and was greeted with acclaim.

Launched in 1979 with a Matisse sketch and the wholehearted support of the family, masterminded from start to finish by Deborah Gage, financed by the amazing generosity of many, and carried out with the expertise and dedication of dozens, finally this project was complete. It was rightly described as 'one of the most difficult and imaginative feats of restoration current in Britain'.

Epilogue

This September, walking slowly alone round the house, which I had not seen since the period when the rooms, empty of furniture, had been stripped down to the bare plaster, any impulse to judge or criticize what has since been accomplished vanished out of the window. As in a dream, I knew that I had been here before, but time seemed to have been telescoped to nothing, and 'then' and 'now' to have become one. Even the changes which have had to be made, some of them important, aroused more pleasure than shock, more appreciation than criticism. All I had to do – and all I wanted to do – was to enjoy: the only reaction that approached the critical was the realization that, in Vanessa's day, the house had never attained its present state of polish and cleanliness but, like any housewife, I saw no great harm in that.

The garden also gave me pleasure, even if here the spirit of perfection had stolen a slight march on that of the *laissez-aller* that used to rule the roost. This must, I think, be inevitable, due to the fact that time is needed for moss and lichen to recolonize the walls, and for rain to discolour the brick edgings. The plants were of course more prosperous and more profuse than of old, and their colours perhaps a little yellower and less blue than Vanessa would have liked; but then, it was September, and these are nuances which will undoubtedly be corrected. The most important thing is that the encouragement, as well as the will to adapt, is so evidently there.

The principle behind everything has been to maintain the very fine distinction between preservation and restoration, the one implying a stultifying metamorphosis into something that is thenceforth beyond change, the other an effort to prevent decay with a tact that is all but unnoticeable. Those who have worked at Charleston have had the almost impossible task of preventing life from claiming its due, in the form of dust and ashes, and coaxing it to remain, in material that was never thought of, by the artists themselves, as inveterately permanent. Miraculously, their spontaneity, not to say their evident indifference to posterity, has stimulated the workers to undertake their task in a new spirit, respecting not only the obvious and the tangible, but something far more difficult to define, the essential atmosphere.

As we wander and gaze at the amazing mixture of richness and economy that make up the interior – riches which have nothing to do with gilt and mahogany – it is not only Vanessa's and Duncan's personalities that become almost tangible, but a way of life. It was a normal, homely family life with the emphasis on pleasure and spontaneity, on work as a healthy solution to life's problems, and on the generous assumption of a certain creativity in all who came there. Even if the family friends did not all sketch, decorate pottery or do embroidery, they often arrived bearing gifts chosen to amuse rather than impress, some of which still remain, adding to the profusion of disparate, unrelated objects, which in any other setting might seem painfully incongruous. At Charleston however, the strangest of confrontations become humorous, or reveal unsuspected affinities. It is perhaps in this aspect that Duncan and Vanessa show themselves as most modern.

This is no doubt because, as artists, their visual instincts took precedence over any more conventional view. It is this that gives Charleston its special character and value, since it is rare to find a house where artists both lived and worked, usually in the humblest of media, leaving behind them a reflection of singular transparency, as though the air still quivered with their presence. It is a house one might visit again and again, without feeling bored by the *déjà vu*, or irritated by a superficial conformism.

In the most obvious sense, the past is irrecoverable, and can no more be lived, except vicariously. While this has its limits, it is instructive, and helps to give us a sense of proportion, to look back. More important is the fact that this glance over our shoulders gives us a sense of continuity: knowing what we come from enables us to guess more surely where we are going, and even to inspire us to make discoveries we might otherwise never have thought of. To my mind this is one of the main reasons for ensuring, with precisely that mixture of enthusiasm and insight so far shown by all who have worked there, that Charleston remains its inimitable self.

Angelica Garnett
Ongles, 1987

Charleston today, blooming and ready to receive visitors

Appendix

The house was originally constructed with a local, vernacular timber frame and the entrance was on the south side where the back door is now. Radical changes were made to the interior and exterior at the very end of the eighteenth century. During the occupancy of Vanessa Bell and Duncan Grant outbuildings were attached to the house, the studio was added and the large window put in the attic. The report below, prepared by David and Barbara Martin of ROHAS, describes, as far as is possible from existing evidence, the structure of the house when it was first built in the late seventeenth or early eighteenth century.

Location Charleston Farmhouse is situated at a height of roughly 42 metres above sea level at the foot of the Downs, 1.2 miles east of West Firle church. It is constructed with its present-day main range set on a NNE–SSW axis, which will be called for ease N–S. Its principal façade now faces east, though the south facing range may formerly have housed the principal rooms.

Layout An 'L' plan house consisting of two 6.5 metre wide ranges each of two and a half storeys. The east facing range runs N–S with a 16.08 metre façade; the south facing range is aligned E–W with a 13.23 metre façade. In the angle between the two is a small two and half storey range which probably housed the staircases. A lean-to formerly ran along the remaining rear wall, which was later replaced by a two storey range. The room at the east end of the south range was originally the kitchen with a massive fireplace located within a four flue axial stack. To the west of this was another heated room, slightly larger but with a smaller fireplace. The function of this room is unclear as is that of the two unheated rooms at the northern end of the east range. The general layout of the ground floor was repeated both on the first floor and in the attic; the attic had 700 millimetre side walls.

Wall Design The principal east and south façades are of coursed flint rising from a neatly formed chamfered brick plinth with brick quoins. The west wall of the south range is of similar construction and continues for a short distance along the north wall, where it ends, 1.4 metres to the west of the 'staircase wing', with a brick quoin. The chamfered stops, at the ends of the crossbeams, are embedded in the flint walls, which shows these walls were original. Also the principal post, at the corner of the north wall, is set against the inner face of the eastern flint façade. All the other external walls were

originally timber framed. Although now hidden by modern rendering, much of the tim-
bering of the north end of the east range survives and was recently found and recorded
(see page 47). It is small-panel type and many of the original staves which carried the
daub infill remain. All internal partitions, including those behind the old lean-to, are of
small-panel timber framing, though little of this is now visible.

Windows Only in the west wall of the south range are original window openings visible and even these have been modified. At first floor level these have brick jambs and
a flat brick arch. No window frames have survived.

Doorways It is not possible to be certain about the position or construction of any original doorway below the attic level. Those in the attic are plain with square heads.

The technical terms used in the sections on the Floors and Ceilings and the Roof
are illustrated on page (142).

Floors and Ceilings All joists span east to west and are supported by intermediate
crossbeams in the south range and girders in the east. All visible crossbeams and
girders in the north chamber are chamfered and have stops, mostly the barred-and-
hollowed type but in the north chamber they are cyma type. All are ornamented with a
raised triangle between the chamfer and the stop. Most joists are now masked by plas-
tered ceilings, but those over an inserted staircase in the west chamber are exposed and
measure 100 mm by 120 mm in section. The lower leading edges have very narrow
chamfers. For some unclear reason the girder in the ceiling of the north chamber on the
first floor is off-centre towards the west. It is not known whether this is replicated on
the ground floor because the details of the ceiling in the north room are hidden.

Stairs The present staircases are modern and have been inserted through existing floors.
As stated earlier it seems likely that the original stairs were in a small wing between the
two main ranges. Traces of the quarter landing of a staircase can be seen rising above
the cellar steps, although even this does not seem to belong to the earliest period.

Roof Both the west and north terminals of the roof are hiplet design without collars at
the apex. At the intersection between the two ranges the roof turns through 90° by means
of hip and valley rafters of irregular cross section, connected by a diagonally set collar.
The roof is mainly constructed with staggered butt purlins, although at least three of the
bays incorporate butted side purlins with continuous common rafters, probably in addition to butt purlins. Modern ceilings mask some of these details. There is evidence of
a trim in the east slope of the south facing range for a dormer window and there may
well have been more such openings in the roof.

Trusses D and F, in the north end of the east facing range, show slightly off-centre door jambs which trim the tiebeams. At their eastern end these trusses incorporate long dragon-ties of uncertain date, whose purpose was to strengthen the wallplates by resting on the flint façade. Truss A, immediately to the east of the axial chimney, incorporates a doorway which trims the tiebeam and also has the remains of daub-filled small-framed panelling. Truss C to the west of the chimney was not closed and queenposts trim the tie beams a short distance in from the walls.

The main roof incorporates an intermediate truss E which coincides with the centre-line of the 'staircase wing'. From this truss two heavy hip rafters extend down to wallplate level. As in the main range the roof of the 'staircase wing' is of butt purlin construction. It has a gabled west terminal with two queenposts but no collar.

Chimney The original axial four-flue chimney survives although much altered. It is of brick construction with its flues aligned along the axis of the roof. Of the four flues only the one serving the kitchen shows any original details and even this has been skinned and narrowed down on the southern side to make room for a passage. But it does retain its heavy, slightly cambered lintel. It is possible that in the space to the south of the chimney there was originally an oven or a boiler.

Quality and Decoration It is a substantial and well built house which incorporates standard construction techniques. The principal post at the west end of the north wall has a square cut jowl while the jowl on at least one other principal post is splay-cut. The timbers are of average dimensions for a building of this size and age. The only surviving décor is the quite elaborate chamfer stops on the crossbeams and girders. Standard assembly is used throughout most of the house except in the intersection of the two ranges where the wallplates are set in level assembly.

Later Alterations The house was extensively modernized in 1796–7 when £537 19s 3½d was spent on improvements. The alterations included adjusting the layout of the ground floor, adding new windows and doorways in the south and east ranges and inserting a new chimney in the north end of the east range. A northern wing, extending westwards from the east range, which replaced the lean-to, may also have been built at this time. Other additions and changes have been made over the years.

David and Barbara Martin
ROHAS
A voluntary organization for the study of historic architecture in East Sussex

Ground plan

East façade

South façade

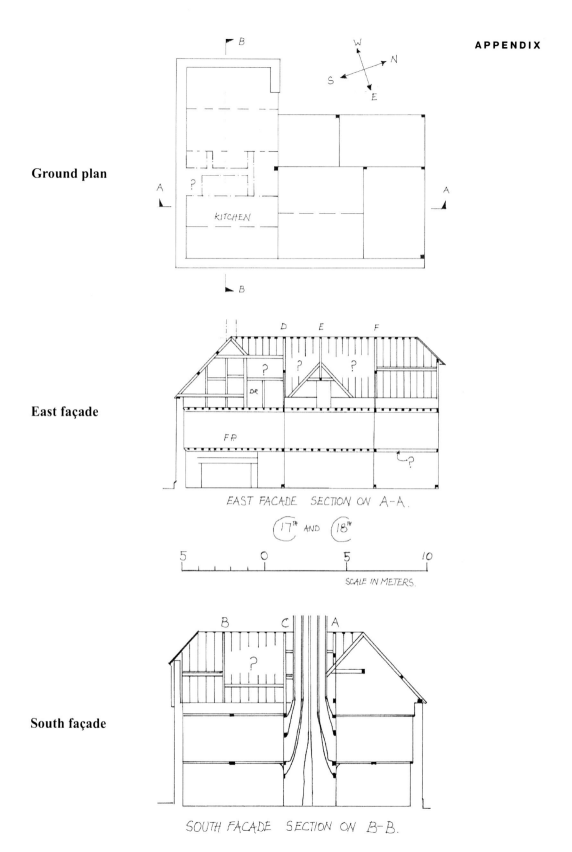

EAST FACADE   SECTION ON A-A.

17ᵀᴴ AND 18ᵀᴴ

5   0   5   10

SCALE IN METERS.

SOUTH FACADE   SECTION ON B-B.

North façade

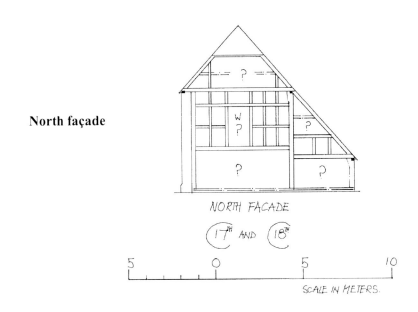

NORTH FACADE

17ᵀᴴ AND 18ᵀᴴ

5   0   5   10

SCALE IN METERS.

Glossary of principal terms

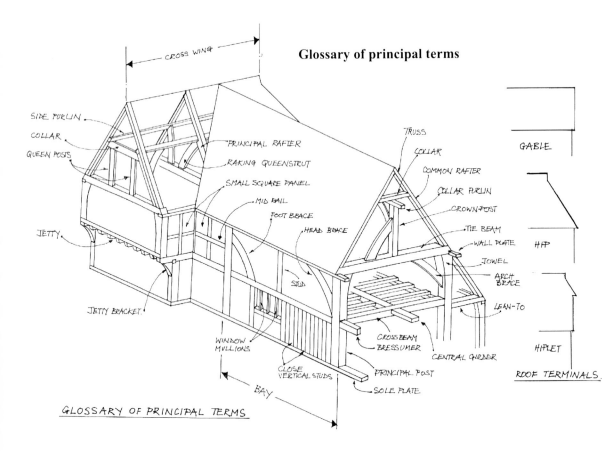

GLOSSARY OF PRINCIPAL TERMS

Acknowledgements

My thanks, of course, go to Deborah Gage. Reading the huge body of her correspondence over the ten years of her involvement with this project has been a privilege and a pleasure. Her energy and attention to detail were phenomenal. She has filled in gaps, answered my questions and encouraged and helped me without in any way interfering with the way I wanted to tell the story.

My thanks to all the people who did the work on the house and its contents, who wrote about it and whose words I have used. (I have given the women the names they had in 1987.) They are: Nicholas Ashley, Penelope Bardel, Corinne Bennett, Danielle Bosworth, Michael Brundle, Joe Dawes, Mark Divall, Geraldine Guest, Wilma Harper, Nick Hunt, Sara Lee, David and Barbara Martin, Elaine Ogilvie, Pauline Plummer, Diana Reich, the late Sir Peter Shepheard, Phillip Stevens, Ann Stocker, Cindy Watts, H.F. Wilson, Heather Wood and the late Alan Younger. My apologies to those we have been unable to contact for lack of a current address. If they would like to contact me c/o Robert Hale I will send them a copy of the book as a token of my gratitude.

My thanks also to Simon Watney and Angelica Garnett for permission to use their extensive contributions; to Olivier Bell for allowing me to quote from Quentin Bell's letters and to reproduce the photograph of the two of them in the garden; to Henrietta Garnett for generously allowing me to reproduce the three paintings by Vanessa Bell; to Anna Fewster who has allowed me to use her photograph of the outside of the house; to Penelope Fewster who has allowed me to use her photograph of the plaque in the garden; to Michael Lovitt for the line drawings; to Richard Shone, Tony Bradshaw and Giles Waterfield who read the manuscript; to Sarah Hall for compiling the index; to Vanessa Curtis who has given me invaluable advice, support and encouragement; and to John Hale, Victoria Lyle and all the others at Robert Hale who have worked on the book.

Last, but far from least, my thanks to Tony Tree. For many years he photographed all that happened at Charleston. He scanned the slides and photographs for this book. His warmth, help and expertise were invaluable.

All photographs except those mentioned above, were taken by Deborah Gage or members of the team who did the restoration and conservation.

Paintings by Vanessa Bell: *Self Portrait* (Courtesy of the Charleston Trust 2010); *Angelica Seated at the Charleston Studio Door* (Private Collection USA); *The Dining Room Window, Charleston* © Henrietta Garnett.

Index